I0410886

REENTRY PARTNERSHIPS:

A GUIDE FOR STATES & FAITH-BASED AND COMMUNITY ORGANIZATIONS

Jamie Yoon
Jessica Nickel

Council of State Governments Justice Center
New York, New York

This project was supported by Grant No. 2006-RE-CX-K005 by the Bureau of Justice Assistance, Office of Justice Programs, U.S. Department of Justice, and Contract No. DOLJ061A20353 (No. 4604-CSG-001 with KRA Corp.) with the Center for Faith-Based and Community Initiatives, U.S. Department of Labor. Points of view or opinions in this document are those of the authors and do not represent the official position or policies of the U.S. Department of Justice, U.S. Department of Labor, or Council of State Governments' members.

Cover design by Farah Assir. Interior design by David Williams.

Suggested citation: Yoon, Jamie, and Jessica Nickel. *Reentry Partnerships: A Guide for States & Faith-Based and Community Organizations*. New York: Council of State Governments Justice Center, 2008.

CONTENTS

FOREWORD

GOVERNORS AND STATE LEGISLATORS ARE JOINING FEDERAL GOVERNMENT leaders in focusing unprecedented attention on the millions of people released from state prisons and local jails each year. State policymakers are concentrating in particular on the handful of neighborhoods in their states that receive the majority of people who have been recently incarcerated.

Constituents in these communities know that the lack of affordable housing, drug and mental health treatment, jobs, and positive role models undermines efforts to make individuals' transition from corrections institutions to the community safe and successful. Although government plays an important role in trying to address these problems, it cannot take them on alone. Service providers based in the neighborhoods where people released from prisons and jails return know best how to access local resources to help former prisoners rejoin communities and families in positive ways. Many times, faith-based and community organizations have the only resources available to help people released from incarceration. They are a tremendously valuable partner if government agencies can better engage them in prisoner reentry efforts.

Across the country, state policymakers have recognized for many years the challenges associated with bridging the gap between large state government bureaucracies that want to facilitate prisoner reentry and small nonprofit service providers intimately familiar with the fabric of the communities where services and supports are based. State departments of corrections and faith-based and community organizations working in the area of prisoner reentry, for example, have distinct cultures, maintain few mechanisms for routine communication between one another, and face other barriers that often make it difficult to partner effectively.

Recognizing the need for a national effort to clarify these challenges and to provide concrete strategies for addressing them, the board of directors for the Council of State Governments (CSG) Justice Center initiated a dialogue with leaders at the U.S. Department of Labor and the U.S. Department of Justice. The result of those discussions was a proposed guide in which the federal government, together with the CSG

Justice Center, could advance efforts by state governments and faith-based and community organizations to partner effectively to improve outcomes for people released from prisons and jails.

Reentry Partnerships is a practical guide for state government officials and representatives of faith-based and community organizations who want to create and sustain collaborative efforts to reduce recidivism and to help people returning home lead productive and law-abiding lives.

As state legislators, we know the costs—to individuals' lives and in taxpayer dollars—are too high to allow prisoner reentry work to fail. The success of these efforts depends in large part on effective partnerships between government agencies and faith-based and community organizations. And as cochairs of the *Reentry Partnerships* advisory group and members of the CSG Justice Center board, we hope this guide will be a valuable resource for all those who work to create and sustain these partnerships.

Senator Stephen Wise
Florida Senate

Assemblyman Jeffrion Aubry
New York State Assembly

ACKNOWLEDGMENTS

THE COUNCIL OF STATE GOVERNMENTS JUSTICE CENTER THANKS THE BUREAU of Justice Assistance (BJA), Office of Justice Programs, U.S. Department of Justice, particularly Director Domingo S. Herraiz and Associate Deputy Director for Justice Systems Andrew Molloy for their enthusiastic support for this project. Thanks are also due to Secretary Elaine L. Chao and the U.S. Department of Labor for their commitment to improving reentry initiatives through meaningful community partnerships. In addition, Scott Shortenhaus, Deputy Director for the Center for Faith-Based and Community Initiatives at the U.S. Department of Labor, has shown unflagging support for this project. Their collective leadership and guidance have been critical to the success of this effort.*

Justice Center board members New York Assemblyman Jeffrion Aubry and Florida Senator Stephen Wise gave generously of their time and expertise. The project also benefited greatly from the advice of Justice Center consultant Elaine Mbionwu, who contributed important information and valuable feedback throughout the development of this guide.

In addition, the Justice Center would like to thank former Commissioner David Donahue, Indiana Department of Corrections; former Secretary James R. McDonough, Florida Department of Corrections; Thomasina Hiers, Maryland Department of Public Safety and Corrections; Carolyn Harper, Public/Private Ventures; Richard Ramos, Latino Coalition for Faith and Community Initiatives; Jane Brown, Virginia Department of Social Services; Tommie Dorsett, InnerChange Freedom Initiative; and Kevin Gay, Operation New Hope, for providing invaluable perspectives on the practical challenges facing collaborations between state governments and faith-based and community organizations.

*The titles and affiliations of the individuals recognized in the acknowledgments were current as of the date this publication was sent to print.

Further, the Justice Center staff would like to thank all of the individuals whose thoughtful experience and expertise are reflected in this publication. In particular, the authors are indebted to the members of an advisory group that convened in June 2007 in Miami, Florida (see appendix A) and participants of the focus group meeting held in April 2008 (see appendix B), who helped formulate strategies for overcoming challenges to collaboration and provided insightful feedback on a draft of this guide.

The authors are extremely grateful to Justice Center staff who contributed to the publication. Director Mike Thompson helped shape the direction of this guide and frame its many complex issues. Blake Norton, Law Enforcement Project Director, provided valuable guidance largely drawn from her experience in the field. Thanks are also due to Communications Director Martha Plotkin for her work in revising and editing this guide. Kathryn Lynch, Communications Associate, assisted in strengthening this guide through her copyediting skills and attention to detail. A special thank-you is extended as well to Sara Paterni, who conducted countless interviews for this guide while working for the center.

Finally, numerous faith-based and community providers and state and local government officials from jurisdictions across the country participated in interviews to provide candid information for this guide. Without their input, the guide would not have been possible. Any value this resource has for the field is largely due to their contributions.

INTRODUCTION

MARK IS A 31-YEAR-OLD MAN WHO HAS SERVED SEVEN YEARS IN PRISON FOR robbery charges and has been incarcerated twice before for possession of a controlled substance. Mark was granted parole but does not have a place to live and is looking for shelter space or will be staying with past associates who still use drugs. Mark has no money and no marketable job skills or training. He does not know who to turn to in order to stay clean, find a stable job, and succeed in the community.

Mark is one of a record number of people being released from prisons and jails in the United States. In 2006, more than 710,000 people were released from state and federal prisons, and approximately nine million were released from jails.[1] Many of these individuals relapse into a life of crime once they are back in the community. More than two-thirds of people released from prisons are rearrested for new offenses within three years of their release, and more than half return to prison for committing new crimes or violating the conditions of their release.[2] Improving the likelihood of people succeeding in the community requires the availability of treatment and programming in correctional facilities followed by reentry services and holistic support in the community. However, providing services that address the wide-ranging needs of people like Mark is a task that state governments interested in reentry cannot tackle alone.

Some states are demonstrating how these high rates of reincarceration can be reduced by providing housing, employment, substance abuse, case management, and other services. These states share a key strategy: they have learned how to create valuable partnerships with faith-based and community organizations that provide reentry programs and services.

Faith-based and community organizations (nonprofits, grassroots organizations, churches, ministries, other houses of worship, and their affiliated bodies) can supply critical services to people released from prisons and jails. In some jurisdictions, faith-based and community organizations may be the only resource for this population. They offer shelter, housing services, food, clothing, employment training, substance

Examples of Faith-Based and Community Organizations' Successes

THE INNERCHANGE FREEDOM INITIATIVE (IFI) is a faith-based reentry program that operates in six states across the country. The program begins 18 to 24 months before an individual is released from prison and provides ongoing mentoring and support for 12 months after release. An independent evaluation of IFI found that program graduates were less likely to be reincarcerated within two years of release than those who did not complete the program (8 percent vs. 36.3 percent).[3]

The Safer Foundation is a large nonprofit organization that administers two minimum security male residential transition centers on behalf of the Illinois Department of Corrections. A study completed in 2004 found that the three-year recidivism rate for the entire group of individuals released from the department in 2000 was 54 percent. In contrast, the recidivism rate for clients of the Safer Foundation who received employment services and attained employment was 21 percent.[4]

Ready4Work is a three-year pilot program that operates in eleven major cities across the country. Ready4Work is administered by the U.S. Department of Labor, Center for Faith-Based and Community Initiatives, and it is jointly funded by the U.S. Department of Labor, U.S. Department of Justice, Public/Private Ventures, and a host of private foundations. Ready4Work provides employment-focused programs, which incorporate mentoring, job training, job placement, case management, and other reentry services, to people released from state prisons. According to Public/Private Ventures, only 6.9 percent of program participants were reincarcerated in state prisons as a result of a new offense within one year of their release.*

---

*Chelsea Farley and Wendy S. McClanahan, "Ready4Work in Brief: Update on Outcomes; Reentry May Be Critical for States, Cities," *P/PV in Brief* 6 (2007), www.ppv.org/ppv/publications/assets/216_publication.pdf. Although these statistics are promising, note that a random assignment study has not been performed, so no strict control group exists for the sake of comparison.

use and mental health treatment, mentoring opportunities, and countless other supports. Faith-based and community organizations also have established ties with individuals and families in their neighborhoods. In particular, staff and volunteers at these organizations have been successful at fostering positive and lasting relationships with people released from prisons and jails. These kinds of relationships can be strong motivating factors for people to engage in reentry programs, seek ongoing support, and remain committed to rejecting a life of crime.

Yet garnering long-term partnerships between faith-based and community organizations and government systems that may not have experience working together—or have had negative interactions—can be a formidable challenge. State policymakers have had little guidance on how to foster and sustain these important relationships. This guide is written to help policymakers and their potential partners make better use of existing community resources and increase their capacity to help people released from prisons and jails succeed in the community.

THE GUIDE

Who Should Read It?

This guide offers practical recommendations for administrators of corrections and community corrections agencies, legislators, and others interested in how their state can improve reentry, reduce recidivism, and build or improve collaborations with community-based service providers. Although the primary audience for this guide is state-level government officials, local government leaders, such as city council members and law enforcement professionals, may also benefit from these strategies. Alternatively, potential reentry partners in the community may find the guide

The Role of Intermediary Organizations

To collaborate with faith-based and community organizations, government officials must address the cultural, operational, and geographic gaps between government entities and community-based providers. Intermediary organizations can be helpful resources for governments seeking to bridge these gaps. For example, intermediaries can interface with smaller grassroots organizations, provide training sessions, monitor performance, and obtain feedback on behalf of states. Intermediary organizations include, but are not limited to, larger nongovernmental organizations, national faith-based and secular organizations, coalitions of organizations, and offices or positions within state agencies specifically tasked to work with faith-based and community groups.

valuable for approaching state and local officials. Highlighted throughout are actions that faith-based and community organizations can take that complement state efforts to improve collaboration.

Impetus for Its Development

The Bureau of Justice Assistance, Office of Justice Programs, U.S. Department of Justice, and the Center for Faith-Based and Community Initiatives at the U.S. Department of Labor have supported the development of this guide in recognition of the growing interest at all levels of government in the role of faith-based and community organizations in prisoner reentry. In January 2001, President Bush created the White House Office of Faith-Based and Community Initiatives and Centers for Faith-Based and Community Initiatives (Centers) in five government agencies. Since then, seven additional Centers have been created.* These Centers have contributed to a national effort to help faith-based and community organizations strengthen and expand their role in providing reentry services to people released from prisons and jails. In addition, more than 30 states have established liaison positions or entities within the governor's office or other state agency to help build partnerships between state governments and faith-based and community organizations.[5] Many more mayors and other local government leaders have reached out to these organizations to help provide reentry services.

Despite these efforts, obstacles to everyday collaborations remain. The momentum generated at the executive level can be sustained only if state agencies and local governments establish policies and practices that address barriers to forging and maintaining partnerships with faith-based and community organizations. As the number of individuals released from prisons and jails continues to increase each year, the demand for reentry services will grow as well. Government agencies must find new ways to work with community providers to meet the service needs of this population. However, few resources exist in the field that describe how faith-based and community organizations and state governments can improve collaboration around reentry, and the roles that each entity can play in this endeavor. This guide is meant to help fulfill this need.

Ensuring the Practicality of Recommendations

To ensure this guide would be of value to policymakers and practitioners interested in reentry, the Council of State Governments Justice Center staff interviewed corrections administrators and other state officials, local government leaders, administrators of faith-based organizations, community-based service providers, and representatives

---

*The 12 federal agencies that have established Centers for Faith-Based and Community Initiatives are the Agency for International Development, Corporation for National and Community Service, Department of Agriculture, Department of Commerce, Department of Education, Department of Health and Human Services, Department of Homeland Security, Department of Housing and Urban Development, Department of Justice, Department of Labor, Small Business Administration, and Department of Veterans Affairs. For more information on the White House Faith-Based and Community Initiatives and its Centers, see www.whitehouse.gov/government/fbci.

of large nonprofits and intermediary organizations. In addition, the project staff conducted a review of published research and relevant materials used in the field. In particular, staff drew on the many recommendations provided by the *Report of the Re-Entry Policy Council.** In June 2007, the Justice Center also convened a day-long advisory group meeting of policymakers and leaders of faith-based and community organizations in Miami, Florida (see appendix A). Meeting participants identified barriers to successful collaboration and strategies for overcoming them. In April 2008, a smaller focus group of state corrections administrators and leaders of faith-based and community organizations, some of whom participated in the earlier advisory group meeting, convened to guide this effort based on their firsthand experiences building reentry partnerships (see appendix B).

Every jurisdiction is unique, and the manner in which the recommendations put forward in this guide are implemented will vary significantly. States must analyze the dynamics between community stakeholders and government agencies at all levels, and address the distinct set of challenges to collaboration.

Common Obstacles to Collaboration

This guide provides strategies to address five areas in which governments often encounter obstacles to collaboration.

Networks. States often lack familiarity with service providers at the local level and have difficulty identifying new partners. To the extent states work with local groups, they often are limited to partnering with just a few larger organizations that are particularly savvy at connecting to government agencies. The absence of an inclusive service provider network can limit a state's ability to connect to community resources.

Funding. Organizations often anticipate cumbersome paperwork and confusing application requirements when contracting with state agencies or competing for grants. Yet grant and contract administrators in state agencies often feel there is little they can do to simplify solicitations while still adhering to funding regulations.

Distinct organizational cultures. State agencies and faith-based and community organizations often have different values, goals, and institutional cultures. A lack of awareness and workable solutions to address these differences can present significant challenges when these two types of groups work together inside correctional facilities or in the community.

Target population. Effective reentry initiatives must respond to the characteristics and needs of the local reentry population. However, some states have found it difficult to identify faith-based and community organizations that are able to work with

---

*The Reentry Policy Council brought together more than 100 leaders from across the United States to develop bipartisan recommendations for policymakers to use to improve the likelihood that adults released from prisons and jails will avoid crime and become productive, healthy members of families and communities. These recommendations were published in January 2005 and can be viewed as a free download at www.reentrypolicy.org. The Reentry Policy Council is a project of the CSG Justice Center.

certain groups in their jurisdiction, especially people at high risk of reoffending or who have special service needs.

Accountability. Tracking outcomes is critical for evaluating the impact of any reentry initiative and for its long-term survival. State funding and other support may be contingent on demonstrating that investments in reentry services are being used wisely. Yet organizations are not always able to measure the effectiveness of their programs and the extent to which they achieve the stated goals.

In the subsequent sections, a goal is presented to address each of these five core challenges. Each goal is then followed by a set of recommendations for state governments and community organizations. Also highlighted throughout the text are innovative programs and city, county, and state approaches to improving collaboration that policymakers can consider when they develop or enhance reentry initiatives.*

---

*Though the examples illustrate a range of strategies that certain jurisdictions have undertaken to improve collaboration, they are not intended to be considered as "best practice" models.

Glossary

Evidence-based practices: Programs or practices that have proven to be successful through empirical research and have produced consistently positive results.

High risk: A term that describes individuals who are likely to recidivate based on factors such as criminal history, attitudes toward crime, unemployment, poor family relationships, mental health concerns, and substance abuse status.

High severity: A term that describes crimes that are serious or violent in nature. These crimes are typically felony offenses, but there is variation across states as to what crimes fall into this category.

Intermediaries: Nongovernmental organizations, national faith-based and secular organizations, coalitions of organizations, or offices or positions within agencies specifically tasked to work with faith-based and community groups as liaisons between local service providers and government entities. They typically have an established organizational infrastructure and a history of working with government. They can act as fiscal agents for smaller groups, and in many cases, they offer training and technical assistance to faith-based and community organizations. United Way, Goodwill, and Catholic Charities are examples of intermediaries.

Logic model (or program model): According to the Office of Justice Programs, U.S. Department of Justice, a logic model is "a graphic representation that clearly lays out the logical relationships between the problem to be addressed, program activities, outputs, and outcomes." The model depicts how a program will work by outlining the sequence of program activities and how these activities are linked to the results that the program hopes to achieve (see http://ojjdp.ncjrs.gov/grantees/pm/glossary.html#logicmodel).

Recidivism: The rate at which people released from prisons and jails commit new crimes, violate terms of probation or parole, are rearrested, or are reincarcerated.

Reentry: The transition individuals make from prison or jail to the community.

Reentry services: The programs, supports, and services people making the transition from prison or jail to the community typically need in order to succeed. These can include, but are not limited to, housing, employment, case management, and substance abuse and mental health treatment services. For the purposes of this guide, these services are directed to people involved in the criminal justice system, including people who are incarcerated and preparing for release, people who have been released from prisons and jails to be supervised in the community, or people who have timed out.

Technical assistance: Training and support that are tailored to a specific organization and its needs. Technical assistance may address a range of topics aimed at improving the effectiveness and efficiency of programs and services provided by the recipient organization.

Timed-out (or maxed-out): A term that describes a situation where individuals convicted of crimes serve the full length of their sentence in prison or jail and will be released unconditionally without any community supervision.

GOALS
AND
RECOMMENDATIONS

Build and Sustain Comprehensive Networks with Faith-Based and Community Organizations

GOAL 1

STATE OFFICIALS HEAR REPEATEDLY ABOUT THE MANY INDIVIDUALS AND organizations ready to work inside corrections facilities and to assist people recently released from prisons or jails. Yet state leaders traditionally have had limited success linking with these community-based service providers beyond those who already have a history of partnering with government. Likewise, faith-based and community organizations that provide reentry services are often unsure what opportunities exist for collaboration and how to connect with government agencies.

Rich networks that include faith-based and community organizations and government entities provide a structure for all members to interact easily. Established networks also help engage individuals and organizations in reentry service delivery and attract nontraditional partners with the capacity to provide needed services— broadening the base of resources that governments can tap into to help people released from prisons and jails successfully return to the community. These networks are also critical for implementing all of the other goals in this guide.

Faith-based and community organizations often establish networks for such purposes as sharing information, building consensus, broadening service availability, and advocating for certain causes. These *formal* networks have leadership bodies that typically coordinate activities through mailings, newsletters, and other dissemination methods and through regular meetings. Relevant networks do not necessarily need to be a statewide or local reentry initiative to provide services to people coming out of prisons and jails. They can be statewide professional associations, such as the Kansas Association of Addiction Professionals. They can be coalitions among certain religious or ethnic groups, such as the North Carolina Council of Churches. They may represent a collection of groups focused on a particular city or county, such as the Boston TenPoint Coalition. In addition, networks can be made up of organizations that focus on a specific issue, such as those in the Los Angeles Coalition to End Hunger & Homelessness.

Government leaders can also look to *informal* networks to find people and organizations that can provide reentry services. One service provider, case manager, or clergy member could maintain a virtual rolodex that enables him or her to bring together key service providers in a particular community. For example, the Ulster County, New York, Probation Department has a long-standing relationship with the New Progressive Baptist Church's Save Them Now program, which provides reentry services. Staff and administrators of the probation department frequently reach out to the church's minister to identify community resources and local service providers.[6]

A smaller number of networks have been established expressly to connect people and organizations that work on corrections and reentry issues. For example, the Alaska Coalition for Prisoner Re-entry is a network of government agencies and faith-based and community organizations that help individuals integrate back into society. The coalition holds regular meetings to identify barriers to reentry, discuss the service needs of the local reentry population, and formulate strategies for addressing these needs. This and other reentry-specific networks present a ready-made collection of people and organizations that are already committed to helping people released from prisons and jails succeed in the community.

The following recommendations outline some of the many strategies that state agencies and faith-based and community organizations can employ to identify these various types of existing networks.* They also suggest ways to involve new individuals or groups in these networks and ways to keep members engaged for the long term. The following section details the need to track and record these networks in ways that facilitate the state government's efforts to work with their community partners. Although not explicitly directed at local government officials, they can use many of these strategies as well to expand county- or citywide networks of providers serving people released from prisons and jails.

*The TPC Reentry Handbook: Implementing the NIC Transition from Prison to the Community Model is another resource for a wide range of stakeholders involved in supporting successful reentry. The Handbook has a detailed description of the variety of teams and partnerships involved in this work, along with examples of team charters, workplans, typical membership, and even suggested agendas and progress reporting formats that might assist in forming and supporting the networks addressed in this document. The Handbook can be accessed on the NIC Information Center web site at http://nicic.gov/Library/022669.

RECOMMENDATIONS

1 | Identify existing networks.

In every community there are networks of individuals and organizations that provide services—such as substance abuse treatment, job training, and mentoring—that people returning from prisons and jails need. State officials, however, are oftentimes only aware of a small number of these networks' members. These state officials can use the following strategies to increase their awareness of potential partners:

- Leverage the connections of other state agencies
- Tap the networks that local governments maintain
- Identify effective intermediaries

State officials can look to other government agencies' networks to leverage the services and resources their members provide. For example, state departments of labor often are responsible for administering employment programs to residents, including people returning from prisons and jails. These state departments of labor typically work closely with trade associations that have their own networks through which information is available about special programs and preapprenticeship opportunities that might be appropriate for people released from prisons and jails. Similarly, corrections administrators—as well as leaders of faith-based and community organizations seeking contacts and resources beyond criminal justice agencies—can reach out to officials in state departments of health, education, transportation, and family assistance. These departments may have information about other organizations that offer services that people released from prisons and jails need, but are not specifically targeted to this population.

Missouri Department of Corrections and Department of Social Services
The Missouri Department of Corrections (DOC) coordinates with the Department of Social Services (DSS) to connect with DSS's Community Partnerships grantees. Community Partnerships are coalitions of local nonprofits that provide services and support to people in need, including people released from prisons and jails. DOC administrators invite Community Partnerships grantees to participate in DOC's regional reentry steering team meetings, which are also attended by probation and parole officers. At these meetings, parole and probation officers can identify local providers and learn about available resources within the community to make better referrals for their supervisees.*

*The DOC convenes monthly steering team meetings as part of the Missouri Reentry Process. Each regional steering team's mission is to integrate successful reentry principles and practices in state agencies and communities resulting in partnerships that enhance self-sufficiency, reduce recidivism, and improve public safety. Members include the Missouri Board of Probation and Parole (part of DOC); Departments of Mental Health, Economic Development, Health and Senior Services, Social Services, Revenue, and Elementary and Secondary Education; and the Office of State Courts Administrator. In addition, the community is represented by treatment providers, law enforcement, city and county government, children of incarcerated parents, victims, and ex-offenders.

Networks that a state agency maintains may span the entire state, but they typically lack depth in individual cities and counties. In contrast, many local government agencies and jails have cultivated extensive networks with service providers within a particular community, but not many beyond their borders. State agency officials should reach out to local government representatives to identify organizations that are, or could be, serving individuals released from prisons and jails. Leaders of faith-based and community organizations also can work with local officials to learn about other groups working in their neighborhoods.

Returning Citizens Public Health Center (Michigan)

Administered by the Bureau of Substance Abuse Prevention, Treatment, and Recovery in Detroit, the Returning Citizens Public Health Center is part of an extensive network of local government agencies and community-based organizations that work together to provide reentry services. It acts as a conduit for state and local agencies to gather information from the network. The Detroit-area community coordinator for the statewide Michigan Prisoner Reentry Initiative (MPRI) sits on the center's advisory board. This allows the state to easily identify local providers and tap the wealth of information available through this network. The MPRI community coordinator works closely with administrators of the bureau and other advisory board members to build relationships with local providers and incorporate them into statewide networks via MPRI listservs, e-newsletters, and directories.

Many intermediaries also maintain networks that may include organizations already providing services to individuals released from prisons and jails and their families. They typically have permanent staff experienced in working with government agencies and have the capacity to conduct outreach to maintain diverse contacts, find new service providers, and continually update listservs and directories (see recommendation 4). Leaders of faith-based and community organizations should also look to intermediaries to identify potential partners in the community and expand their own networks of known providers.

Faith and Service Technical Education Network (National)

The Faith and Service Technical Education Network (FASTEN), a collaborative initiative originally coordinated by The Pew Charitable Trusts, involved the National Crime Prevention Council, Harvard University, the Sagamore Institute for Policy Research, and the Baylor University School of Social Work. Acting as an intermediary, FASTEN sponsored research and a number of conferences as well as a major website at www.FASTENnetwork.org. FASTEN's focus was on multi-sector collaboration for community transformation. Although its primary audience was always faith-based practitioners, it also sought to assist public officials—including state government representatives—and staff from philanthropies in understanding faith-based social service and connecting faith leaders to these sectors. Pew's financial support ended in 2005, but the website continues, now overseen by Sagamore Institute. The website has expanded to include a large number of resources for congregations desiring deeper involvement in their communities. The site offers several resources for practitioners engaged in reentry.

2 | Expand networks to include faith-based and community organizations not already working with government entities.

After compiling a list of relevant networks, state officials and community leaders should concentrate on establishing and deepening relationships with new partners. To incorporate providers not already connected with statewide networks, state officials can conduct the following activities:

- Attend local reentry-related meetings
- Convene forums in the community to engage local providers in reentry service delivery, especially in neighborhoods where people released from prisons and jails often return*
- Leverage the knowledge of parole and probation, and law enforcement officials who are familiar with local service providers
- Ensure that agencies are working with a wide variety of providers, such as faith-based organizations (from different faith traditions) of varying size, diverse community-based organizations, and those both new and experienced in serving the community

State officials can attend opening ceremonies for new halfway houses or attend kickoff meetings for local initiatives to show support for organizations that have yet to establish a relationship with the state or reinforce existing relationships with local providers. To find out about these meetings, state agency staff should monitor community calendars, listservs maintained by state and local governments as well as intermediaries, relevant websites, and bulletins administered by local nonprofits.

Once state agency leaders have identified events and meetings to attend, they should make every effort to send an agency representative with suitable experience and authority. In many cases, it is appropriate for staff from regional offices of state agencies to attend local meetings because they typically are more familiar with area service providers and their activities. Other agencies send community relations teams to represent the state at relevant gatherings. After staff members have attended multiple meetings in a particular community and have developed or enhanced relationships with local service providers, agency administrators should continue to send them to represent the state in that community to ensure continuity and foster trust.

Court Services and Offender Supervision Agency (Washington, DC)

The federal Court Services and Offender Supervision Agency (CSOSA), which oversees individuals who are on probation, parole, or supervised release in Washington, DC, employs six community relations specialists who maintain strong, active relationships with key stakeholders in local neighborhoods. The community relations team coordinates Community Justice Advisory Networks in each police district. These networks are made up of residents, businesses, faith-based and community partners, school officials, community-based service providers, and

*In every state there are a handful of "high-stakes" communities to which most people released from prisons and jails return. See Council of State Governments Justice Center, *Justice Reinvestment Overview*, http://justicereinvestment. org/facts_and_trends.

local government and law enforcement officials. The community relations specialists convene regular meetings with network members to address community members' public safety concerns directly and identify resources that are available to CSOSA's client population. The community relations specialists also represent the agency at regular meetings and events organized by local agencies, nonprofit organizations, and neighborhood associations.

In addition to attending meetings hosted by local organizations, state agency officials can convene their own forums—particularly in areas in which many people released from corrections facilities return. These should be open-door meetings and should include faith-based and community organizations of varying size and experience working with government agencies. States should encourage grantees and other partners to recruit new groups to attend these discussions. Agency staff should solicit participation from communities and service sectors that are underrepresented in existing networks or at past meetings.

Topeka Reentry Roundtables (Kansas)

In an effort to reach out to faith-based, volunteer, and community organizations and individuals working with people released from prisons and jails, the Kansas Department of Corrections convenes monthly meetings in Topeka. These meetings offer informational sessions with guest speakers and panel groups that focus on different reentry themes. Participants have the opportunity to ask questions and discuss how these issues are playing out in their neighborhoods. New participants also learn about available resources and supports that can help them serve their clients and can link to networks of organizations already attending community meetings and coordinating services. To attract a diverse group of attendees for these meetings, department administrators contact organizations from various service areas (such as housing, employment, and substance abuse) and encourage them to participate and bring along representatives from new organizations. Administrators circulate sign-up sheets among participants, and new participants are encouraged to be involved and are included in contact lists maintained by the department.

At these meetings, state officials should clearly articulate the mission and goals of the agency as well as the purpose of convening the meeting. Service providers should know what to expect from the state and whether they can anticipate future funding opportunities. State officials should lead a concrete discussion about their strategy for improving delivery of services to people released from prisons and jails. It is important to outline specific goals, a plan for meeting these goals, and the role faith-based and community organizations can play in an initiative. To reach organizations that are unable to attend, agency staff can post meeting minutes or Q&A highlights on websites and in electronic mailings and enable community members to respond to the group on meeting topics. Faith-based and community organizations will approach this work with varying missions, some focused on fundraising, others on direct service. It is advisable for states to weigh the mission, goals, and objectives of each partner as they forge relationships at the community level.

Parole, probation, and law enforcement officers who work directly with people released from prisons and jails can also be good resources for state officials seeking to build a network among faith-based and community organizations. For example, state officials can encourage directors of county probation departments to compile the names of organizations and individuals that probation officers have worked with in the past. This information should then be folded into department or statewide lists of providers, so that knowledge accumulated by staff in the field is accessible to agency administrators. Information can flow in both directions: lists can also be circulated within county probation departments, so that officers can tell individuals under their supervision about available community programs.

Family Assistance Project, South Dakota Federal Probation Office
Through its Family Assistance Project, the South Dakota Federal Probation Office provides referrals to its sizable Native American client population for services and supports in the Sioux Falls community. Probation staff conducts interviews with representatives from numerous local agencies and community-based organizations to identify resources available in the community for housing services, substance abuse treatment, employment assistance, and other areas. In addition, they informally share information from these lists with state and local community corrections agencies during joint trainings and community-wide conferences and events, and in situations where the Federal Probation Office and state or local community corrections agencies are supervising the same individual.[7]

In all of the networking activities that are conducted, it is critical that there be sufficient diversity among the groups. While larger organizations are better known to state agencies, it is important to expand contacts with smaller entities and individuals who provide important services and supports to people released from prisons and jails as well. Government agency staff should be certain that there is also representation among different faiths in the networks that are being built and that experienced providers are continually being asked to identify and welcome new participants.

3 | Keep networks active and invigorated.

After identifying and expanding existing networks, state officials must work to ensure that they do not grow stale or stagnant. A network's true value depends on how engaged its members are: Do the leaders of the network convene people regularly around substantive issues? Is there strong attendance at these meetings? Do the members ensure their activities are consistent with a clearly articulated mission? Are regular updates provided to members via mailings, listservs, and web postings?

To encourage faith-based and community service providers to be active members of local and statewide networks, state leaders should engage in the following activities:

- Promote networks as a vehicle for sharing and accessing information
- Use networks as a forum for connecting members and government officials
- Designate the staff and allocate the resources needed to maintain relationships with members of networks

State officials and network administrators should encourage active participation by allowing members to disseminate their announcements about upcoming meetings, calls for presenters, new facility openings, and other relevant information. They should also ensure that updates and meetings provide valuable information to members. For example, state officials can provide timely information about state requests for proposals (RFPs) and other funding opportunities. In addition, they should use various outreach strategies to alert all contacts about training sessions and workshops as well as opportunities to receive technical assistance. State officials also can provide network participants with user-friendly highlights of recent research and developments from the field.

Nonprofit Coordinating Committee of New York, Inc.

The Nonprofit Coordinating Committee of New York, Inc. (NPCC) is a membership organization that offers a number of resources of interest to organizations providing services to people released from prisons and jails. It publishes a monthly newsletter and provides updates on legislative and regulatory developments affecting the state's nonprofit sector. It also conducts workshops on management issues such as developing effective boards, working with volunteers, and preparing for audits. NPCC maintains a website with timely articles and updates on upcoming events, trainings, workshops, and funding opportunities.

People will also remain engaged in a network when they sense that it improves their access to people they might not otherwise meet or see. Network participants can initiate relationships with key decision makers in state and local government and in the community. These relationships create a foundation for meaningful collaboration. For example, a state official planning a reentry initiative can identify key community leaders who can provide insight on how state funds could best respond to the needs of people released from prisons and jails. A reentry service provider can connect with an influential agency administrator, who can suggest potential partners for a future grant proposal or recommend well-respected government officials, local leaders, and organizations to provide a letter of support.

Sacramento Valley Regional Care Coalition and the
California Department of Corrections and Rehabilitation

The Sacramento Valley Regional Care Coalition, a multiethnic, multidenominational coalition of churches and nonprofits that provide social services in the region, has developed a close working relationship with the California Department of Corrections and Rehabilitation. Coalition members meet with agency officials regularly to highlight local reentry needs, identify what services coalition members can provide, and discuss the possibility of allocating government funding to fill service gaps. During these meetings, agency officials and coalition members plan collaborative efforts to conduct public education campaigns for projects and initiatives with which they are involved. Furthermore, agency officials have tapped coalition leaders to help coordinate the strategic planning for, and implementation of, statewide reentry initiatives.

Learning about various networks in the community, attending meetings, staying abreast of announcements and updates, and maintaining relationships with key members require substantial staff time. Responding to inquiries from faith-based and community providers, and connecting them to government staff or directing them to other resources, can be time-consuming as well. Too often, these responsibilities are simply added to the responsibilities of a state employee whose to-do list is already impossibly long. To demonstrate the importance of this work, state officials should make building and maintaining relationships with faith-based and community organizations an explicit part of a person's job description and allocate commensurate time to complete the duties, or create specialized positions, such as "community coordinators," devoted to these activities. The extent to which the people in these positions are successfully fulfilling their responsibilities should be measured periodically to ensure continued support for their functions. These measures could reflect answers to such questions as the following:

- How many local meetings did the person attend?
- How many different neighborhoods is the person working in?
- How successful is the person at mapping community providers in the neighborhoods he or she is responsible for?
- How many new providers were added as contacts?
- How long has this person been working with each of his or her contacts?
- How many times was this person able to connect one community-based provider to another?
- Do local providers know this person?
- Is this person credible in the neighborhoods he or she works in?

4 | Create directories.

States that invest staff time building and maintaining relationships with networks and their members also need a way to institutionalize these connections, so that their continued success is not contingent on the involvement of a single individual or team. State officials should ensure that information about service providers and other contacts is readily shared with relevant agencies and the public. Accordingly, many states have created or supported the development of easy-to-access directories—sources for information about organizations providing reentry-related services. Directories can take many forms, such as reentry handbooks, resource guides, and online databases. Web-based and print directories can facilitate appropriate referrals and service-delivery coordination more effectively. They can also help states meet community needs by better identifying the range and capacity of local resources and gaps in services in particular neighborhoods.

There are two critical, yet often overlooked, steps that must be taken to ensure directories will be useful:

- Incorporate providers from a broad range of diverse backgrounds
- Create effective mechanisms to routinely update entries

Directories should reflect the full range of services and providers in the community. State officials developing directories can employ the strategies described earlier in this section to identify and include organizations beyond those already working with them. They also can disseminate surveys through the newsletters, mailings, and listservs of various organizations and their contacts to gather information. State officials may also want to establish criteria for listing providers in directories. Any rules that govern exclusions should be carefully detailed, and instructions for submitting new entries should be clearly described for both web and print directories. These directories should be made available to the public, so that service providers can make better referrals and individuals released from prisons and jails and their families can identify providers and obtain services.

SHARE Network (Missouri)

In 2006, the Missouri Department of Economic Development, Division of Workforce Development, partnered with the U.S. Department of Labor and other state and local agencies to develop a statewide comprehensive social service resource directory called the SHARE Network. This web-based directory is free and available to the public. More than 5,200 nonprofit organizations, educational institutions, government agencies, and for-profit providers are listed. Organizations that choose to join SHARE Network must accept its member agreement, which includes criteria for membership and a description of the review and approval process for provider entries.*

Directory information can quickly become outdated, and revising and verifying each entry can be time-consuming and costly if state staff members are responsible for these tasks. For print versions, states must allocate staff time and funding or enlist other organizations such as intermediaries to refresh directories, typically on an annual basis. Web-based directories, however, can be revised on an ongoing basis, and updated listings can be made available to the field instantaneously. The use of volunteers to update and verify information can greatly reduce the costs of maintaining directories and allow states to provide a more useful resource to the field.

Community Transition Coordination Network (Washington)

4People is an online information and referral service for Washington State's 39 counties. This nonprofit organization compiles information about social services and resources for the Community Transition Coordination Network. It maintains a database of government, nonprofit, and faith-based direct service providers in the state. Users of the 4People website can complete an online form that solicits information about available programs and services and submit information to be included in the directory. The task of verifying information, which can be the most time-consuming component of maintaining a directory, is delegated to volunteers. 4People disseminates a request for "virtual volunteers" to verify information on providers and services in the database and compile lists of necessary changes for the 4People staff to upload on the website. Service providers are also encouraged to call or e-mail 4People staff about any changes that need to be made about their listing.†

---

*For more information on the SHARE Network, see www.sharenetworkmo.org.

†4People is maintained through local grassroots efforts but includes local, statewide, and national resources. Also available is a tool that helps case managers connect and coordinate reentry services from a range of agencies and organizations, including the Department of Corrections, employment services, housing providers, mental health treatment providers, food pantries, and shelters. In addition, 4People provides self-help tools for families to identify service needs and connect to resources available through its directory. For more information about 4People, see www.4people.org.

GOAL 2

Simplify Pathways to Funding for Reentry Initiatives

ALTHOUGH STATE AGENCIES AND OTHER POTENTIAL FUNDERS CAN PROVIDE information through their established networks about grants and other relevant opportunities, faith-based and community organizations often require guidance to navigate the application process. State agencies' grant solicitations, in particular, may have rigorous requirements that applicants must meet. The request for proposals also may be hard to understand and time-consuming to complete, which often discourages faith-based and community groups from pursuing these funding opportunities. Many perceive these cumbersome processes as bureaucracy at its worst. For their part, state officials see themselves as simply complying with regulations that they did not institute and cannot change. State agencies will need to work with the organizations in their networks to simplify solicitations and application processes whenever possible— for both grants and contracts.*

The recommendations that follow focus on how state agencies can work within existing regulations to simplify their solicitations. They also suggest ways in which faith-based and community organizations might benefit from assistance developing competitive proposals, including partnerships with other entities. These strategies can help faith-based and community organizations improve their ability to respond to solicitations not only from state governments but also from federal and private funders, and to sustain their efforts over time.

---

*Some funding agencies distinguish between grants and contracts by whether the original source of funds is external (a federal agency or foundation) that is administered by the state, or from the states' own budget, respectively. Other policymakers and practitioners use these terms loosely. Because both grant and contract recipients can subcontract to a faith-based organization or other entity, this document distinguishes between the terms only when it is necessary to highlight differences in grant or contract qualifications, accountability, reporting, or other requirements. For the purposes of this guide, community and faith-based organizations that receive funding directly from state agencies will be referred to as *grantees* or *contractors*. Community and faith-based organizations that receive funding through an intermediary or other organizations whether from a grant or contract will be referred to as *subcontractors*.

RECOMMENDATIONS

1 | Ask faith-based and community organizations how solicitations and application processes can be improved.

Before releasing the next solicitation for proposals from faith-based and community organizations interested in providing reentry services, state administrators should request advice from a cross-section of these organizations' representatives on how to improve it. Ideally, state agency officials would convene meetings to discuss this feedback. Important questions to ask include the following:

- *What language and terminology were difficult to understand?*

  Solicitations often contain complex guidelines and technical phrases that can limit the applicant pool to candidates who are already well-versed in fundraising and developing successful proposals. Such terms as *revocation rates, criminogenic needs, performance metrics,* and *match money* may be unfamiliar to staff of some organizations and thus discourage these groups from responding to the proposal. States may wish to simplify solicitations to encourage a larger pool of applicants.

- *What application requirements were difficult to understand or meet?*

  Potential applicants also may be unsure about how to meet specific requirements listed in solicitations. For example, providers may be required to conduct formal risk and needs assessments, but they may not know which instruments are validated for the criminal justice population or how to obtain and administer them. Another common concern is that certification requirements for staff administering programs are often difficult for faith-based and community organizations to fulfill (discussed more fully in recommendation 2 below).

- *What aspects of the submission process could be improved?*

  In addition to the content of the solicitation, administrators should also review the proposal submission process. Solicitations sometimes require short turnaround times, creating challenges for those applying, especially for organizations new to this process. Government agencies often require applicants to obtain a standard tracking number before they can submit a proposal, and they accept only a certain application format or electronic file type for these proposals.

- *Are the funding range and time frame presented in the solicitation appropriate?*

  The funding amount offered in solicitations should be sufficient for organizations to meet the expectations for service delivery, but states may not have an accurate sense of what activities the funding award amount will support in a given contract or grant period. In some cases the funding amount might be too small to adequately cover the costs needed to deliver the services described in the solicitation.

In other cases, the funding amount might be too large and unmanageable for smaller organizations, so that they would be excluded unless options for subcontracting or other partnerships with the primary grantee or contractor are outlined in the solicitation.

The funding period also should be considered when developing grant programs or contracts. If state agencies provide multiyear funding, grantees and contractors may be more able to provide long-term programs and services without disruptions caused by gaps in funding. This is particularly important for smaller organizations without large reserves to cover the lag time between securing different grants or contracts or between winning a grant award or contract and receiving the first installment of funds.

In working through these questions, representatives of faith-based and community organizations may gain a better appreciation for the limited flexibility of state agencies when developing a solicitation. State officials can use information collected from this process to improve future solicitations and ensure that the language is written in such a way that encourages new providers to compete for available funding. They also can identify specific trainings and supports that applicants need, and that states should invest in, to help them complete applications.

2 | Assist faith-based and community organizations in meeting licensing and certification requirements.

Many solicitations require that licensed professionals provide or supervise programs or components of programs consistent with the state's licensing and certification standards within their particular field of work. Mental health and addiction professionals, including psychiatrists, psychologists, social workers, and certified alcohol and drug counselors, may be needed to deliver certain services. State officials should consider whether proposed requirements inadvertently filter out or discourage capable groups from submitting proposals. While these standards are important and cannot be lowered, they may be impossible for some nonprofits to meet with their existing staff—even if they have the substantive expertise. State administrators should develop options and strategies that would allow these organizations to apply for funding and comply with licensing and certification standards.

Several approaches to facilitate participation may be considered. States may encourage organizations to obtain licenses or accreditation by offering financial incentives, such as making it a condition for receiving additional funding or renewing a grant or contract. If this approach is taken, states should also consider setting aside some funding, such as a small stipend, to help organizations cover the costs of getting licensed or certified.

States also can make adjustments to RFPs by disaggregating components or tasks that require licensed professionals from those that can be implemented by community organizations' staff alone. Applicants would only propose to work in the areas in which they are permitted. Alternatively, states can leave the proposals as a single solicitation and encourage faith-based and community groups to contract with licensed or certified providers to deliver specific program components. To ensure the subcontractor has the right qualifications for the required services, state officials may want to review or help write descriptions of duties for the certified or licensed subcontractor. When solicitations *allow* faith-based and community organizations to contract separately with licensed or certified providers, states must offer adequate funding for these arrangements.

3 | Assist faith-based and community organizations in developing competitive proposals and managing grant awards.

Faith-based and community organizations must dedicate significant resources to respond to solicitations and develop proposals—in many cases only to see their proposal rejected. Leaders of organizations often become discouraged by the application process and disengage themselves and their organizations entirely. Other organizations try repeatedly for funding but continue to take the same missteps. To help organizations that were not provided funding to improve their chances for an award, and to encourage peer-to-peer learning, some state grant or contract administrators connect them with successfully funded entities. These grantees' representatives may also be able to encourage those who have given up in the past to reengage in the process.

Faith-based and community organizations debating whether to respond to a state agency's request for proposals, particularly organizations that have repeatedly sought but failed to receive government funding, may benefit from individualized technical assistance. Intermediaries as well as state agencies offer training and tailored assistance to faith-based and community organizations. Some intermediaries go so far as to help potential applicants draft proposals and submit applications (see recommendation 4 below).

Ohio Department of Rehabilitation and Correction, Office of Policy and Offender Reentry
The Ohio Department of Rehabilitation and Correction, Office of Policy and Offender Reentry, offers a variety of trainings and support to help individuals and organizations interested in applying for federal, state, and private funding.* It helps potential applicants improve their proposals before submission by reviewing the application, assisting in writing the proposal, and providing letters of support. Staff works with potential applicants to ensure, among other things, that proposals adhere to the RFP, fit the mission and vision of the department, and can produce measurable outcomes.

*In cases where funding is offered through the Ohio Department of Rehabilitation and Correction, staff and administrators at the Office of Policy and Offender Reentry do not participate in the selection process.

Local Initiatives Support Corporation (national)

With support from the U.S. Department of Justice, the Local Initiatives Support Corporation (LISC) coordinates the Community Safety Initiative, which seeks to improve public safety and build long-term partnerships among police departments, community developers, and community members. As part of this project, LISC provides technical assistance to help community partners identify funding opportunities from public and private entities and respond to solicitations. LISC staff meets with individuals from partner organizations to formulate program goals and logic models, ensure their proposal responds to the service priorities articulated in solicitations, and reviews and edits draft proposals to send to funders that LISC helped to identify.[*] Services are free to faith-based and community organizations, and LISC promotes these technical assistance opportunities through various local networks and reentry councils with which they have existing connections.[†]

For some faith-based and community organizations, everyday demands make it impossible to find time to receive needed training on responding to funding solicitations and on developing the infrastructure to meet application requirements. In these cases, state officials may consider offering small capacity-building grants or stipends—or directing applicants to other private and public entities that provide them. Such grants can help smaller faith-based and community groups develop the skills necessary to formulate solid proposals and offset some of the costs of building their organizational capacity. These grants can be used not only for grant proposal writing but also to improve program planning and development, financial management, and technical infrastructure. The overall goal of these grants is to help recipients get to a point where they can develop proposals on their own and meet basic application requirements.

OneStar Foundation, Compassion Capital Fund Texas Demonstration Project

As part of the 2005 Compassion Capital Fund Texas Demonstration Project—and in collaboration with project partners Cornerstone Assistance Network, the Urban Alternative, Venture CD, Baylor University, and the Texas Health and Human Services Commission—OneStar Foundation administered capacity-building grants for 25 faith-based and community organizations. Grant awards ranged from $1,500 to approximately $29,000 per grantee organization for proposed capacity-building projects. Eligible applicants included faith-based and community organizations with an operating budget of less than $500,000 that provide social services to people in need in Bexar, Harris, Tarrant, and Travis counties and had attended at least four of six capacity-building symposia/workshops offered in their region. Grantees underwent an initial assessment process to identify their specific needs related to organizational capacity, and based on the results, grantees then created logic models for their capacity-building projects. OneStar reviewed and approved these logic models and guided the implementation of proposed activities. OneStar and project partners also conducted group trainings and provided individualized technical assistance on topics such as fiscal accountability, strategic management practices, board development, and evidence-based service delivery. Grantees were required to submit quarterly reports and a final

---

[*]See the glossary for a definition of *logic models*.

[†]For more information on the Community Safety Initiative and the technical assistance LISC provides, see www.lisc.org/section/areas/sec1/safety.

report on progress they made toward the intended outcomes outlined in their logic models, as well as documentation for reimbursement for approved capacity-building activities.

Some more established organizations that have had success winning grant awards and contracts (and thus may not be eligible candidates for capacity-building grants) could still benefit from less intensive support on managing awards and contracts and streamlining operations. State agencies can administer periodic training sessions for current or potential grantees and contractors as part of an ongoing effort to improve the quality of services available to people released from prisons and jails. States can also contract with private consulting groups, larger nonprofits, and intermediaries to provide this type of training and technical assistance.

Nueva Esperanza, Inc. (Pennsylvania)

Nueva Esperanza, Inc. is a faith-based community development corporation that serves as an intermediary to help faith-based and community organizations improve their ability to provide social services. In 2002, Nueva Esperanza contracted with the Pennsylvania Department of Community and Economic Development to work with 12 providers operating in two jurisdictions, Reading and Allentown, as part of Nueva Esperanza's larger Hispanic Capacity Project. These 12 providers received technical assistance in the form of daylong training events held three times per year, facilitated by expert consultants. Training topics included (1) fundraising—creating a development strategy, writing grant applications and reports, building a development staff; (2) leadership—building an effective board of directors; (3) financial management—budgeting, cost allocation, setting up a computerized accounting system; (4) program development—designing effective programs, strategic thinking, ensuring sustainability; and (5) communications—developing a web presence, creating a marketing plan.

4 | Encourage some faith-based and community organizations to subcontract with intermediaries that could reduce the burden associated with pursuing, receiving, and administering grants and contracts.

Some faith-based and community organizations that provide first-rate services may come to the conclusion that the time they spend developing proposals and administering grants and contracts is an inefficient use of their resources and talents. Leaders of organizations often become resigned to working with existing funding because they perceive the states' application process to be unlikely to result in new support. Even when these organizations do receive funding, they may be overwhelmed by the administrative tasks that are associated with financial reporting and tracking program activities. In all of these instances, it may make sense for the faith-based and community organization to consider subcontracting with an intermediary, which can absorb the tasks associated with developing a competitive proposal and complying with funders' reporting requirements if and when funding is obtained.

In these arrangements, the intermediary will be responsible for writing and submitting a proposal and will be the primary recipient of funding. The organization(s) that will be doing the actual work in the community will be considered the *subcontracting organization(s).** Whenever possible, a subcontracting organization and the intermediary should meet to clarify the terms of the agreement prior to submission. The proposal should explain what activities the intermediary will complete, what the subcontracting organizations will complete, and how funds will be divided among the parties. If a subcontracting organization is not identified at the time of submission, the proposal should explain what activities the intermediary plans to delegate to the subcontractor and how the award would be allocated.

Once a contract or grant award is made, the intermediary is responsible for making sure that all services that were promised are delivered. The intermediary typically conducts all the administrative, financial reporting, and oversight duties. The intermediary must establish a separate agreement with the subcontracting organization, regardless of whether this organization was specifically named in the proposal, that details how the faith-based and community group will provide the services required under the primary contract or grant. It should also identify when and how the intermediary will pay or reimburse the faith-based and community organizations for their work.

Intermediaries should work to ensure that the subcontracting faith-based or community organization indeed has the capacity to provide the services that are promised. For their part, staff and administrators of faith-based and community organizations must understand their cost of delivering services. They should come to the negotiation informed and prepared and should first take the time to assess their own financial status, analyze and estimate expenses for administering a program, and be able to demonstrate that their services are evidence-based and effective.

Once a subcontract is established, faith-based and community organizations will need to provide the intermediary with periodic reports. The intermediary must then compile this information and format it to meet reporting requirements for the funder. Many intermediaries provide training, technical assistance, or administrative support to subcontracting organizations on data collection and reporting.

Black Ministerial Alliance (Massachusetts)

The Black Ministerial Alliance (BMA) is a coordinating entity for a group of more than 80 faith-based and community organizations that engage in advocacy and provide direct services to individuals in need, including people returning to the community from prisons and jails. BMA acts as an intermediary by obtaining grants from government and private funders and subcontracting with faith-based and community organizations that offer direct services. BMA reimburses faith-based and community organizations in monthly installments for various costs associated with providing programs and services to clients. The faith-based and community organizations receive tailored technical assistance and training to help them meet reporting requirements. They submit regular reports directly to the BMA, which then compiles information into reports for funders.

---

*In some cases, these organizations may be referred to as *subgrantees* rather than *subcontractors*.

Faith-based and community organizations may not be familiar with intermediary organizations or know which ones they can enter into contracts with to obtain funding. State grant or contract administrators should identify a range of intermediaries that are able to serve in this capacity and are also willing to take referrals from states. Administrators should then compile a list of these intermediaries and share it with faith-based and community organizations that may be interested in entering into subcontracting arrangements.

Conflicts between the intermediary and subcontractors about the terms of the subcontract sometimes occur. Smaller organizations may feel the intermediary they are working with is not sharing funds appropriately. Intermediaries may be frustrated to learn halfway through the grant period that their subcontractors simply do not have the capacity to serve the number of clients agreed to in the subcontract. It is in the best interest of the state and other funding agencies to try to avert or help resolve these conflicts.

When awarding a grant or establishing an agreement that names one or more subcontractors, states may want to conduct a mandatory training session with both the intermediary and subcontractor(s). These trainings can highlight potential problems that often occur between the parties, offer strategies for overcoming these challenges, and promote frequent and regular communication about grant or contract activities. When conflicts cannot be averted through training, state officials should work to mediate the situation and help guide the parties to a resolution.

5 | Front-load grant awards and contracts.

Unlike large, well-established nonprofits, small faith-based and community organizations receiving an award often do not have the resources to make the up-front investment required to launch a program. Expenses associated with recruiting and hiring staff and purchasing necessary equipment and supplies sometimes exceed an initial installment of award funds. Reimbursable contracts, which force program administrators to wait several months before the first reimbursement check is processed, can create significant obstacles for these smaller organizations.

To address this problem, states can use "draw-down" awards or contracts if allowable in the funding program, which allow a larger portion of the total funding award to be spent at the beginning of the contract or grant period. For example, under a $5,000 "draw-down" grant over a five-month period, the grantee would receive the first $1,000 monthly installment at the time of the award and would submit reimbursement forms for up to $1,000 each subsequent month to cover the cost of administering programs and providing services. Without increasing the total award amount, states can greatly enhance a smaller organization's ability to successfully meet grant requirements by adjusting the payment structure.

Recognize and Understand Distinct Organizational Cultures

LEADERS OF A FAITH-BASED OR OTHER COMMUNITY ORGANIZATION MAY mistakenly assume that with a contract or grant—or even with just an informal invitation—they are ready to begin delivering services inside corrections facilities or in partnership with parole and probation officials. In fact, much still needs to be worked out. Accessing and working in a correctional facility, in particular, often requires some negotiation between the corrections staff and the direct service providers.

Prisons and jails operate under a strict set of policies and procedures designed to protect visitors, the corrections staff, and those people under their supervision. These rules and regulations may sometimes be unfamiliar or confusing to service providers. Often, differences in culture and service approach impede the ability of community-based providers and institutional and community corrections officers to work together. Understanding, respecting, and determining how to bridge these differences are essential components of successful partnerships between community providers and corrections personnel.

The recommendations in this section review how corrections professionals—from both facilities and community-based supervision agencies—can promote information sharing and mutual support between corrections and community corrections staff and providers working inside prisons and jails and with people who are on probation or parole. They suggest ways to create a welcoming environment for faith-based and community representatives and to establish special protocols for working with volunteers inside correctional facilities. They also discuss strategies for managing the interface between service providers and corrections officers and using technology to facilitate service delivery.

RECOMMENDATIONS

1 | **Promote information sharing and mutual support between providers from faith-based and community organizations and corrections and community corrections staff.**

The first priority of community corrections and prison and jail administrators is to protect the public and provide a safe environment for their staff and those they supervise or incarcerate in their institutions. Faith-based and community organizations seeking to deliver services inside prisons and jails must learn how to work in this context. The same holds true for volunteers and staff requesting to serve people on probation and parole.

Corrections employees, particularly uniformed officers, are sometimes unsure of service providers from faith-based and community organizations who want to work with people who are incarcerated or under community supervision. Some of these officers are concerned that providers sometimes can be manipulated—unwittingly becoming potential carriers of contraband or involved in other prohibited activity. Leaders of corrections agencies should address these concerns by mandating that anyone who works inside a secure institution or probation or parole agency participate in orientations and trainings. Some state and county departments of correction already coordinate mandatory orientation sessions to outside contractors and service providers before they can begin working in prisons or jails. These sessions typically include a tour of the facility and explain the background-check process, security regulations, and evacuation procedures, as well as why these rules are needed. Trainings should also include a discussion about maintaining boundaries, physical and otherwise, between people who are incarcerated or under community supervision and the staff of faith-based and community organizations. Staff and volunteers must understand that they should not do favors or engage in relationships that can compromise the safety of the individuals involved as well as an entire facility or others. Corrections staff should plan to periodically review these rules and reinforce them on an ongoing basis.

Corrections officials should also help faith-based and community service providers understand the perspectives of uniformed staff and shift commanders in prisons or jails. Just as corrections staff are trained to be respectful toward visitors and workers who come to their facility, community service providers should be sensitive to the culture among personnel in the prison or jail. Simply being on time, courteous, and appreciative to the men and women who work in stressful conditions every day can go a long way in cultivating positive relationships on which a reentry program depends. Staying power is typically highly valued among corrections staff. The longer an individual or organization provides services, demonstrates commitment, and exhibits professionalism, the more readily corrections staff will accept their presence and integrate community-based services into day-to-day operations. In addition, it is important for staff and volunteers of faith-based and community organizations to understand the organizational dynamics within the institution they are working and know who they should turn to with questions and concerns.

Faith-based and community providers should also reach out to probation and parole officers who are supervising the same individuals they are serving. To this end, providers will need information on a client's supervision requirements and how community corrections officers monitor, encourage, and enforce these conditions. Understanding the conditions of supervision will help in developing a realistic transition plan for the person who is returning to the community. For example, some people on probation or parole may have curfews, which prevent them from accepting employment that requires working past a certain hour. Similarly, a service provider should understand and appreciate how and when a person under community supervision must report to his or her probation or parole officer when considering job placement, housing, transportation issues, and more.

Although frequent communication is important (see goal 4, recommendation 3), regular meetings that involve both corrections or community corrections staff and representatives of faith-based and community organizations can really help break down barriers and enable each party to appreciate the other's perspective. For example, tensions can be generated over the need for officers to conduct surprise visits to those on probation or parole. A candid discussion about the need for such measures can improve working relationships. Administrators of faith-based and community organizations can invite uniformed officers to regular staff meetings for discussions about program goals, the organization's particular philosophy or approach to programming, and the day-to-day challenges of delivering reentry services. Similarly, corrections officials can invite staff of faith-based and community organizations to routine meetings that will expose them to the culture of the agency, its processes and approaches, and why priorities are set as they are.

2 | Create environments inside prisons and jails and probation and parole offices that welcome faith-based and community organizations.

The concept of reentry may seem like a remote idea to some officers in prisons and jails. Corrections administrators should communicate to frontline staff and their supervisors the value of the services that faith-based and community organizations deliver. This message can be conveyed during orientation training for new officers as well as regular staff meetings. Wardens and shift commanders can also explain how programming can increase security—by keeping individuals who are incarcerated occupied and by providing a healthy outlet. The same holds true for the need to communicate to parole and probation officers the tremendous value of involving faith-based and community volunteers and staff.

Corrections administrators should also attempt to formalize agreements with leaders of the partnering faith-based and community organization to advance a shared understanding of a reentry program's goals and design. Faith-based and community organizations should clearly explain the goals of the programs they want to provide inside a correctional facility and on release to the community. They should also state how they plan to implement the program while still adhering to facility security standards and to the needs of community corrections agencies if they also intend to serve prisoners or inmates when they return home. Ideally, these would be established in writing, such as a memorandum of understanding, which both administrators of the correctional facility or agency and the community-based service provider would sign or approve. This is particularly helpful when a provider runs into problems with facility staff that may not be familiar with a particular program or initiative.

In addition, corrections administrators should encourage prison and jail personnel and probation and parole officers to sit in, when appropriate, on a program session that a community-based service provider conducts. Administrators and officers can also attend reentry program recognition or graduation ceremonies. These ceremonies, when attended by both community-based service providers as well as corrections staff, can reinforce the partnership between the two parties that enables in-prison and postrelease programs to function.

Prisoner Reentry Employment Program, San Diego Second Chance (California)
San Diego Second Chance administers the Prisoner Reentry Employment Program (PREP), which provides pre- and postrelease services, including job readiness training and placement, housing, mental health, and life skills programs, to individuals incarcerated in state and county correctional facilities in San Diego. Before launching the program, Second Chance presented facility administrators with a detailed description of the curriculum and program activities and provided supporting research for the program model. To engage corrections officials in the PREP program, staff encourages corrections officers as well as agency administrators to sit in on classes and attend program graduation ceremonies. Second Chance tracks program data such as the number of individuals who enrolled in the program, completed the program, and secured employment upon release, and it submits regular updates electronically to corrections administrators.

Aspects of the corrections agency's background checks, entrance procedures, or other policies designed to maintain safe and secure institutions may impede the work of faith-based and community organizations. Accordingly, corrections administrators should review these policies with service providers to determine the least restrictive requirements that still meet safety standards and other facility or agency needs.

• *Background checks*
  Volunteers or service providers seeking access to the institution or agency may include some people who have criminal records. Having personal experience behind bars can make individuals especially effective in working with people who are incarcerated; such a record should not automatically ban someone from the institution or reentry activities. In such cases, corrections staff can consider

evidence that the person's return to the community has been successful, that prior criminal activity has ceased, and the security procedures established for the institution or agency will be followed.

- *Entrance procedures*

  Entrance procedures for providers who have worked in a facility for five years should not be the same as those required for a first-time volunteer. Corrections administrators should review policies around security checks and may want to consider replacing blanket protocols with a graduated system for granting different levels of clearance. This can help expedite entrance procedures for providers who have worked in a particular facility for extended periods of time and have demonstrated professionalism and willingness to adhere to facility rules.

  ### Security Clearance ID Cards (Maricopa County, Arizona)
  In county correctional facilities in Maricopa County, Arizona, community-based providers that have been approved to conduct in-prison programming are issued ID cards that clearly indicate the security clearance level for that individual. This allows all corrections officers to quickly determine whether individuals should have access to various parts of the facility, and providers can easily enter and exit once they have passed the initial ID screening process.

3 | Establish special protocols for working with volunteers inside correctional facilities.

Volunteers can be a great resource for states seeking to provide reentry services to incarcerated individuals.* They can offer services and assistance that corrections budgets might not otherwise be able to support. Yet even the best-intentioned volunteers can burn out quickly. And if volunteers quit shortly after they begin, investments in their training, monitoring, and programming are lost. Accordingly, both corrections administrators and the faith-based or community organizations with which volunteers are associated must do their part to make sure placements are a good fit for both the volunteer and the correctional facility. Volunteers must be committed to working with individuals on an ongoing basis. State agencies should develop screening protocols to identify volunteers who are truly able to work in a correctional environment. Service organizations should develop mechanisms to gauge their level of dedication and suitability. Some agencies and organizations develop contracts of commitment or establish minimum hourly requirements for volunteers who wish to provide services inside prisons and jails.

---

*It is important to note that volunteers are not substitutes for professionals who are licensed, certified, or specifically trained to deliver programs and services—and not all volunteers are well suited to work in prisons and jails. Most programs need to be provided several times a week, and client-to-provider ratios must be limited to ensure effective service delivery. And, whereas most volunteers offer their time at night and on the weekends, it is during traditional office hours on weekdays that most programming must be provided. See www.reentrypolicy.org/Report/PartI/ChapterI-B/PolicyStatement4/Recommendation4-D#38-note.

Community Justice Project, Greater Minneapolis Council of Churches (Minnesota)

Community Justice Project volunteers who serve as mentors for soon-to-be-released inmates are required to complete a five-hour training, where they learn how to forge positive relationships with their mentees, what rules they must follow within the correctional facility, and how to interface with corrections staff and probation officers. Trainings are co-facilitated by program staff at the Greater Minneapolis Council of Churches (GMCC), corrections and probation officers, and the Minneapolis Police Department. Training sessions are conducted within the Hennepin County Correctional Facility so that mentors can familiarize themselves with the working environment. GMCC has developed a formal job description that details expectations for mentors working inside the facility, and volunteers must make a commitment of four hours per month for a minimum of one year. In addition, facility administrators screen potential volunteers by conducting full criminal background checks.

Though the value of volunteer services cannot be overstated, it is important to recognize that there are some unavoidable commensurate costs that should be anticipated. For example, volunteers require some training about working in a secure facility and about the obstacles that people released from prisons and jails returning to the community face.[8] Volunteers may also need coaching about the elements of services most likely to have an impact on the client, which can be time-intensive. Their work inside correctional facilities must be consistent with the individual's overall reentry planning and programming, which may be coordinated by a team of government and community-based providers. Corrections administrators should clearly explain to volunteers what evidence-based standards are being used for reentry programs, if applicable, and how their work as volunteers fits into this model.

Kansas Department of Corrections, Risk Reduction and Reentry Program

The Kansas Department of Corrections leverages the help of volunteers to implement its Risk Reduction and Reentry Program in correctional facilities and in the community. Volunteers who are recruited are presented with information about the evidence-based plan for implementing risk reduction and reentry services with high-risk, high-need inmates before they begin work. Specific ways volunteers can support and help carry out risk-reduction case plans are spelled out to clarify how their desire to help individuals be successful fits into the overall strategy. Mentors and trainers define the roles and expectations for volunteers and prepare them for the reentry work. To ensure that volunteers adhere to evidence-based practices, these developers and trainers monitor their work and provide ongoing feedback.

Like any other valued resource, a pool of volunteers should be managed effectively, which requires a coordinated plan for training and oversight between the corrections administrators and the community groups that provide the volunteers. To support volunteers who may feel isolated or underappreciated, corrections administrators should work with the organizations to facilitate the formation of support groups. Furthermore, corrections administrators should prominently recognize the important contributions that volunteers make through public events, such as appreciation days, honorary dinners or lunches, or periodic awards.

4 | Manage communications between corrections personnel and representatives from faith-based and community organizations.

Even with orientations, trainings, and other efforts, people on the front lines of corrections and faith-based and community organizations inevitably will experience occasional friction as they work together. Such situations may arise, for example, when there are changes in personnel or when prior agreements concerning a program design or a security protocol are misunderstood.

As discussed in recommendation 1 above, staff should be familiar with the appropriate avenues for raising questions and concerns about working in a facility. Assigning a single point of contact for faith-based and community organizations can help resolve minor conflicts or clarify any confusion about scheduling, security procedures, rules of conduct, and other day-to-day issues. For issues that cannot be resolved by this point person alone, administrators should make clear who corrections personnel and staff and volunteers of faith-based and community organizations should raise concerns to, and establish a process by which these will be mediated and resolved.

Volunteer Coordination Committee, Texas Department of Criminal Justice

The Volunteer Coordination Committee (VCC) administers a statewide program for volunteers serving in the Texas Department of Criminal Justice and is comprised of statewide representatives from its six divisions.* The VCC works with unit chaplains and unit volunteer coordinators who oversee the day-to-day management of volunteers at a particular correctional facility. The unit chaplains are the point of contact for volunteers from faith-based groups and the unit volunteer coordinator is the contact for volunteers not affiliated with a faith-based group. Conflicts with a volunteer or his or her program that cannot be resolved by unit chaplains or volunteer coordinators, wardens, or other facility administrators are addressed by regional representatives. If the regional representative cannot resolve the conflict, the issue is then directed to the VCC coordinator. Formal action in response to perceived misconduct by a volunteer is initiated with a standardized Violation of Policy Form describing the behavior. This form is then forwarded to the regional representative and then to the VCC coordinator for review. Responses to misconduct could involve, among other remedial actions, a letter of instruction, additional training, suspension, or removal from the volunteer program.

Regardless of whether a facility has designated a liaison, the staff and volunteers of faith-based and community organizations working inside prisons and jails should forge a relationship with the shift commander in charge during the time frame they conduct programs. The shift commander typically dictates access and security procedures for his or her shift and often sets the tone for the rest of the officers on duty. The shift commander can be a powerful ally in promoting cooperation between facility personnel and providers.

---

*The Committee is tasked with establishing agency policies, goals, and objectives regarding volunteers; enhancing and coordinating volunteer activities; reporting on these activities; and analyzing critical issues and providing guidance to departments or divisions. For more information, see www.tdcj.state.tx.us/pgm&svcs/pgms&svcs-vlntrcoorcom.htm.

5 | Use technology to enhance community-based providers' ability to deliver services to individuals who are incarcerated.

When community-based providers cannot gain access to a correctional facility to work with individuals, either because the facility is in a remote location or because an individual's security classification precludes contact with outside visitors, corrections administrators should consider possible alternatives for service delivery. Many correctional facilities have been using teleconferencing and video technology, when available, to address these obstacles. These technologies allow faith-based and community organizations to provide services, such as mentoring, vocational classes, and counseling, without incurring the high costs and logistical complications of travel and adherence to safety protocols. They also preclude the need to deal with the problems associated with both transporting and supervising the individual who is incarcerated to receive services off-site.

However, the use of videoconferencing and other technologies should not completely replace face-to-face interactions with people who are incarcerated or under community supervision. Building trust and establishing ongoing relationships with individuals can increase the likelihood that an individual will continue to participate in programming and treatment. When possible, relationships with individuals who are incarcerated should be initiated with direct interactions before the use of remote-access technologies.

Tailor Responses to the Population Who Will Be Served by a Reentry Initiative

MANY REENTRY INITIATIVES FOCUS ON PEOPLE WHO ARE BELIEVED TO BE most likely to commit a new crime or whose acts are so serious that even a small chance of reoffending should be given priority. Studies have found that reentry initiatives that direct their programs and services to people who are at high risk of reoffending have the greatest impact on reducing recidivism.* Corrections administrators assess "risk of reoffending" using assessment tools, which take into account a number of factors such as criminal history, criminal attitudes, employment, family relationships, mental health, and substance abuse status.† Research suggests that directing treatment and programming to people who have special needs, such as those with mental health issues, has a substantial impact on reducing recidivism.‡

To make the most of the reentry dollars they spend, corrections administrators appropriately concentrate their programs and services on individuals at a high risk of

---

*See the glossary for a definition of both "high risk" and "high severity." A study of residential reentry programs that offered cognitive–behavioral or behavioral programming found that those programs that focused on high-risk individuals (more than 66 percent of program participants were high risk) achieved a greater reduction in recidivism (8%) than those that did not target high-risk individuals (−1%). Furthermore, programs that provided high-risk participants with more services over a longer length of stay achieved an even greater reduction in recidivism (18%). See Christopher T. Lowenkamp, Edward J. Latessa, and Alexander M. Holsinger, "The Risk Principle in Action: What Have We Learned from 13,676 Offenders and 97 Correctional Programs?" *Crime and Delinquency* 52, no. 1, 77–93.

†Risk assessment instruments include the Salient Factor Risk Instrument, Static 99, Rapid Risk Assessment for Sexual Offense Recidivism, and Level of Services Inventory—Revised. The Council of State Governments Justice Center has developed an online tool that compiles descriptions of 16 different risk assessment tools, see http://tools.reentrypolicy.org/assessments/instruments/Recidivism+Risk.

‡A three-year felony recidivism study of individuals who participated in Washington State's Dangerous Mentally Ill Offender Program found that the program reduced overall felony recidivism by 37 percent and achieved a $1.24 return for every public dollar spent on the program. Program participants received mental health treatment and additional supportive services for up to five years after release. See Jim Mayfield and David Lovell, *The Dangerous Mentally Ill Offender Program: Three-Year Felony Recidivism and Cost Effectiveness* (Olympia: Washington State Institute for Public Policy, 2008).

reoffending or who have special needs. But the people that states want to prioritize for reentry program participation do not always align with the individuals that faith-based and community organizations are able or willing to serve. State officials are sometimes frustrated that these organizations may seem reluctant or ill-equipped to work with hard-to-serve populations.

Yet faith-based and community organizations often lack the training or capacity to meet grant requirements to serve people who are likely to commit new crimes or violate their conditions of release. People convicted of violent crimes may have a history of gang involvement, which poses some particularly difficult issues. Others who present distinct challenges are people leaving prisons or jails with serious mental illnesses, who are oftentimes homeless. When providers are told that continued funding is contingent on their ability to demonstrate positive outcomes for people receiving their services, they question the reasonableness of the state's expectations.*

To address these concerns, states should create financial incentives for organizations to focus on high-risk individuals and those with special treatment and service needs. States should also provide better support to providers who do serve these populations, and promote information sharing, when appropriate, among government agencies and community-based providers working with these individuals.

---

*Service providers are also pressured to ensure resources are available for people in the community who have not been involved in the criminal justice system and are in need of the same assistance. State officials would benefit from learning more about capacity issues and where there are current gaps in community services.

RECOMMENDATIONS

1 | **Create funding opportunities that help providers specifically focus on individuals who are at high risk of reoffending or have special treatment and service needs.**

States can offer financial incentives, such as specialized grant programs or contracts, to encourage faith-based and community organizations to work with people who are likely to reoffend or have special needs. These funding opportunities can focus on such services as gang intervention, substance abuse and mental health treatment, sex offender treatment, housing placement, and—when appropriate—parenting and family reunification programs. Solicitations should detail the priority population's characteristics and service needs so that community organizations can properly tailor their proposed program designs.

Washington State Re-entry Housing Pilot Program

In 2007, the Washington State legislature passed Engrossed Substitute Senate Bill 6157, which authorized funding for the Washington State Re-entry Housing Program. The program addresses individuals returning from prisons or jails who are at high risk of reoffending, have significant treatment and service needs, or lack a viable housing option upon release into the community. Possible candidates include those with co-occurring substance abuse and mental health disorders. Community-based organizations that receive grants under this pilot program must provide rental assistance and supportive services to program participants. Organizations work collaboratively with the Washington State Department of Corrections to monitor progress, identify any additional programming and treatment needs, and ensure that individuals under community supervision meet the conditions of their release.

Even with funding tied to support for these hard-to-serve individuals, service providers may still be reluctant to respond to solicitations. As mentioned above, some providers are concerned that they will not be able to demonstrate positive outcomes, which in turn could compromise their ability to secure future funding. Because slips and relapses are inherent in the recovery process from addiction,[9] measures other than abstinence will be necessary. For individuals with mental illnesses, changes in behavior (e.g., regular program attendance, medication adherence) rather than changes in symptoms can be measured.[10] States' standards for what constitutes a "successful outcome" must reflect these realities, and measures should reflect the longitudinal nature of the recovery process. Outcomes should emphasize treatment participation, compliance with treatment recommendations, and program completion.

To complement funding, state officials should convene meetings at the local level to learn what additional resources potential grantees and contractors will need to provide effective reentry programs for individuals at high risk of reoffending or who have special needs. Based on that feedback, states should strategically invest in technical assistance, training, and other supports for providers, which are discussed further in the next recommendation.

2 | Provide training and support to faith-based and community organizations on serving high-risk, high-needs individuals.

Faith-based and community organizations may not have staff specifically trained to identify and respond to gang involvement, to conduct risk assessments using validated tools and evaluate the results, to work with individuals with co-occurring mental health and substance abuse disorders, or to provide behavior modification programs for sex offenders. Staff at faith-based and community organizations can acquire some of these skills by attending trainings already offered to the field by corrections agency staff, intermediaries, and private consultants. In other cases, certification or licensing may be required to perform certain functions, and staff can be trained to support the efforts of certified or licensed professionals.

Catholic Charities of Kansas City-St. Joseph (Missouri)
Catholic Charities of Kansas City-St. Joseph coordinates the "TurnAround Program," which offers transitional services to people who are in prisons or on parole. Most program staff members have a background in criminal justice or social work and have the requisite experience to work with high-risk individuals. For program staff and volunteers who do not have this background, Catholic Charities provides on-the-job training on these program participants' service needs and all related safety concerns. Catholic Charities partners with the local diocese and other local reentry service providers working with high-risk individuals to conduct similar trainings for their staffs as well.

State and local laws can severely limit employment and housing opportunities for people with criminal histories, particularly for individuals who have committed serious crimes. They can inadvertently create obstacles to reentry in other ways as well. Service providers who work with high-risk individuals may need to navigate these complex legal mandates. This may require that providers receive technical assistance on how to understand and comply with regulations and laws governing their priority population. For example, faith-based and community organizations serving sex offenders must comply with restrictions that prohibit their clients from living within a certain distance from schools, playgrounds, and parks, depending on the jurisdiction. These restrictions make it difficult for providers to meet sex offenders' reentry needs, such as housing, particularly in urban communities where there are few areas where they can reside. State governments should ensure community organizations receive relevant training and support on how existing laws affect their work and to formulate strategies for serving the population within legal parameters.

Developing a communications plan is another important task for organizations that serve high-risk or high-needs individuals. Some providers may want guidance on how to respond to potential media coverage of negative incidents involving clients. States should assist faith-based and community organizations to develop media response protocols and strategies for proactively educating communities on the myths and facts about people released from prisons and jails, in addition to responding to high-profile incidents. This includes the public safety issues related to their reentry—and to what extent services may be able to increase community safety.

States may also wish to publicly recognize outstanding faith-based and community partners that serve high-risk populations. Highlighting success stories and crediting community partners can help sustain strong working relationships and may also help those organizations in securing additional funding from private donors and foundations.

3 | Facilitate appropriate information sharing among government agencies and faith-based and community organizations working with individuals who are at high risk of reoffending or have special treatment and service needs.

Community-based providers, law enforcement officers, and supervision officers often encounter the same individuals, yet many jurisdictions lack formal mechanisms for information exchanges among them and others in the reentry network. Frequent and regular interaction with community-based providers can help officers anticipate and address any public safety concerns and help ensure individuals meet their conditions of parole or probation.

Montgomery County Re-Entry Collaborative Case Management Meetings (Maryland)
The Re-Entry Collaborative Case Management group meets biweekly to develop case management plans for high-risk individuals who are about to be released from the Montgomery County Correctional Facility. The group is composed of corrections staff (case managers, treatment staff, and a social worker), local law enforcement officers, representatives from parole and probation, human service agency officials, and faith-based and community service providers. The group conducts these 90-minute meetings to coordinate programming and provide an effective continuum of services. Between meetings, the Re-Entry Unit Manager at the correctional facility communicates with members of the group via an e-mail list, providing meeting minutes and updates on upcoming cases to be discussed.

When appropriate, government agencies should share pertinent information with providers working with high-risk individuals, or those convicted of serious and violent offenses, in keeping with all legal mandates. Government agencies must comply with the Health Insurance Portability and Accountability Act of 1996 (HIPAA) regulations and have a full understanding of what kinds of information can be shared directly and what necessitates a waiver signed by the individual. For example, properly providing information on an individual's criminal history, conditions of supervision, and treatment plan can help a reentry provider take the necessary precautions to ensure public safety and place the individual in an appropriate housing arrangement. Though federal laws apply to all, other rules that govern information sharing vary from state to state, and even between jurisdictions. State personnel can educate representatives from agencies and community groups on mandates and help establish internal policies and protocols that facilitate information exchanges.

Ensure Accountability for the Efficient Use of Funds and Gather Critical Data

GOAL 5

THERE IS AN INCREASING EMPHASIS IN STATE GOVERNMENT ON ACCOUNTABIL-
ity and, more precisely, performance measurement. Elected officials responsible for
state budgets, understandably and appropriately, want to know how allocated funds
have been spent. They also want to know the impact of those expenditures.

However justifiable this process is, faith-based and community organizations
often find themselves victims of its unintended consequences. Initially excited to
begin delivering services to their clients, faith-based and community organizations
that receive a state grant or contract frequently find themselves consumed with trying to understand and fulfill reporting requirements. Sorting through the forms and
reports they must complete, these grant recipients are frustrated that their precious
resources are spent administering the grant instead of providing important services.

The recommendations that follow explain the need to clearly identify what
should be measured when a grant or contract is awarded. Next, they discuss how
to minimize the burden that these requirements generate for grantees while providing both the state and the faith-based and community organizations with extremely
valuable data. They offer strategies for organizations to get the most they can from
routine data collection and reporting. Finally, they review the characteristics of studies that will provide policymakers with information they need to determine whether
to continue funding for a program and suggest ways to partner with other entities to
conduct these studies.

RECOMMENDATIONS

1 | Clearly define which measures faith-based and community organizations should use to assess their services.

When state officials enter into an agreement with a grantee or contractor to provide certain services within a particular program model, the parties should agree on which quantifiable measures matter in tracking progress toward desired outcomes and ensure they are reflected in the written agreement. *Process measures* might include tracking the number and type of interventions the service provider made, the timing of these actions, and the number of participants that have completed various progressive stages in the program. In some cases, faith-based and community organizations may not have the capacity to determine outcomes, and indeed conflict of interest issues arise when an organization conducts outcome evaluations of its own programs. (For strategies to overcome some of these challenges, see recommendation 4.)

Once grant and contract administrators have agreed on what information should be tracked, they should then develop a system for how grantees and contractors should capture and report the information. States may want to consider developing standardized reporting forms to facilitate information processing. States also may want to simplify reporting metrics for smaller organizations.

Service Level Inventory, Ohio Governor's Office of Faith-Based and Community Initiatives
The Ohio Governor's Office of Faith-Based and Community Initiatives gathers data on all grants it administers to assess whether program implementation is consistent with the model established in the award. To streamline data collection from numerous grantees, it has developed a Service Level Inventory form, which can be tailored to each grant program. The form identifies eight service areas and lists specific activities that fall under each category. For example, housing is identified as one of the service areas, and grantees must indicate how many people were provided with emergency rental assistance, housing deposits, and temporary housing. Grantees must complete the form monthly and submit it to the grant administrator.

If resources are available, it may be possible to set up a computerized case record management system that not only gives grantees or contractors access to clients' records but can also be used to generate statistical reports. For example, a case record management system should track, among other things, program completion information for each service area and generate statistical reports on the reasons for any terminations. These systems can also facilitate information sharing among program providers and can support subsequent recidivism research or other studies discussed in recommendation 4.*

---

*When computerized systems are not available, a paper-based template can be used, and the information entered into an off-the-shelf database to achieve some of these same benefits.

Although crucial to grant and contract administration, written reports do not provide a complete picture of how a program is implemented by the faith-based or community organization. State officials should consider conducting announced and unannounced site visits, which can be useful in verifying information in written reports and can help state officials gain a better understanding of the day-to-day operation of reentry activities. Site visits typically involve conversations with staff at various levels of the organization, interviews with recipients of services, observation of a class or group session, and review of the service provider's current caseload. If there have been administrative or logistical problems, or they are anticipated, capitalizing on a site visit to resolve them face-to-face can expedite troubleshooting.

Expectations for what information contractors and grantees must track, how this information must be reported, and how compliance with these reporting requirements will be monitored should be clearly spelled out in the grant solicitation and further explained in bidders' conferences, preproposal meetings, and other events where state administrators discuss funding opportunities with potential applicants. Administrators should also communicate to applicants how this information will be used by the state and when, if at all, the results of analyses will be made available.

2 | Help faith-based and community organizations meet reporting requirements.

Although many providers may understand what the expectations are for tracking and reporting information, they still may need help incorporating these activities into their daily work and fulfilling the sometimes time-consuming requirements once the grant or contract begins. States can minimize the onus on providers while ensuring that they get information that can guide decision making about funding particular programs. To minimize reporting challenges, government officials can provide trainings for any organization receiving a grant award or contract from a state agency. Such trainings could address some of the following questions:

- How are standard measurements defined?
- How do you determine who is eligible for services?
- How do you address "double-counting" issues for individuals who receive multiple services?
- How, if at all, do you count services that an individual receives that is not specifically a component of the program funded by the state?
- What constitutes a referral?
- What constitutes a meeting?
- How is attendance in meetings determined? Do late arrivals or partial attendance count?
- How can these new data be used to help improve the reentry program or how it is currently implemented?

Virginia Department of Social Services

The Virginia Department of Social Services (DSS) administers a number of grant programs that provide funding support to faith-based and community organizations serving people released from prisons and jails and their families. All solicitations that DSS issues state that providers receiving funding must complete training on program and reporting requirements within 90 days of the grant award. This training is administered by the Office of Community Partnerships and is meant to ensure that grantees have a uniform understanding of what information about financial, administrative, and program activities must be reported.

Regularly collecting and reporting data is a time-intensive undertaking and will require allocating a portion of a person's time to fulfill these responsibilities. Even with initial training from the funding agency, the staff person charged with this work may need ongoing assistance. The following strategies may help alleviate some of the burden of reporting obligations.

First, state's grant or contract administrators can directly help recipients build administrative capacity and streamline accounting procedures. Second, state agency officials can refer contractors and grantees to nonprofits and private consulting firms that offer this type of training and technical assistance. Officials can also consider working with an intermediary specifically to provide instruction and support in this area to grantees or contractors.

JAE Enterprises, Inc. (Philadelphia, Pennsylvania)

JAE Enterprises, Inc. is a business consulting firm that offers organizational development services and technical assistance to small businesses and nonprofit organizations seeking to build organizational capacity. In 2006–2007, JAE contracted with the Philadelphia Department of Human Services to provide a series of 12 workshops for grantees of the department's Support Community Outreach Program. In addition to providing training on budgeting, accounting, and establishing 501(c)(3) status, the workshops helped grantees learn how to track data about their programs and how to produce accurate reports for funders.

Third, states can contract directly with intermediaries that assume the reporting responsibilities of its subcontractors. The subcontracting faith-based or community organization must provide information to the intermediary that can be used in the reports to the state.

Latino Coalition for Faith and Community Initiatives

The Latino Coalition for Faith and Community Leadership is a national intermediary organization committed to strengthening the capacity, enhancing the programs, and expanding the reach of faith-based and community organizations. The Coalition primarily seeks to work with organizations serving Latino at-risk or adjudicated youth. As an intermediary, it provides funding, technical assistance, and organizational development using a cadre of consultants and on-the-ground city project directors, who are responsible for local implementation, accountability, and coaching of subgrantees. The Latino Coalition employs the "Efforts to Outcomes" software to educate subgrantees on how to collect, enter, and create data reports for all clients served. City project directors then work with subgrantees to ensure that information is properly recorded in the

RESOURCES FOR INTERMEDIARIES
Compassion Capital Fund (CCF), National Resource Center

THE COMPASSION CAPITAL FUND—which is coordinated by the Administration for Children and Families, U.S. Department of Health and Human Services—established the National Resource Center (NRC) in 2002. NRC has developed a number of reports and tools available online for intermediary organizations:

• *National Resource Center E-Newsletter: Best of the Best*
(www.ccfbest.org/)

This website compiles the most useful articles and resources from the NRC's e-newsletter, which is intended as a resource for intermediary organizations funded by CCF, published between October 2003 and September 2005.

• *Toolkit for Faith-Based and Community Organizations*
(www.acf.hhs.gov/programs/ocs/ccf/resources/toolkit.html#gbks)

This toolkit features eight guidebooks for intermediary organizations on a number of topics including establishing partnerships with faith-based and community organizations, managing sub-awards, and delivering effective technical assistance.

• *Breakthrough Performance: Ten Emerging Practices of Leading Intermediaries*
(www.hhs.gov/fbci/Tools%20&%20Resources/Pubs/breakthough.pdf)

This report highlights promising practices of leading intermediaries that have built successful partnerships with faith-based and community organizations and have expanded the capacity of these organizations to serve people in need.

database on an ongoing basis. The Latino Coalition can easily draw statistics from the database for monthly and quarterly reports to the primary funders and can also use the information for subgrantee evaluations.*

3 | Help faith-based and community organizations leverage data collection.

States should communicate to faith-based and community organizations that data collection is not just for the benefit of state officials and it is not solely an evaluation tool. Data collection can be beneficial for faith-based and community organizations because it requires them to develop the organizational infrastructure needed to meet reporting requirements that can help with other aspects of their work. In particular, it encourages staff and administrators of smaller faith-based groups and grassroots organizations to establish systems and habits that will help them to better track bills and payments, articulate program goals, demonstrate a track record of service for future funders, increase professionalism, and improve general office efficiency.

Apart from the indirect benefits associated with the processes involved in data collection and reporting, the data can be immediately useful in determining whether a program is on the right track. Data about program participants that capture demographic information, screening and test results, and attendance records for meetings and classes can help staff determine what adjustments in the program model or implementation are needed.

States should provide or connect faith-based and community organizations to training and technical assistance on how to translate data already being collected for routine reports into useful information about how to improve program models or implementation. For example, an organization launching a GED program for 30 high-risk individuals may discover, after a few weeks of recruiting participants and conducting initial literacy screenings, that the majority of eligible participants are reading at or below the third-grade level and thus not yet ready for GED instruction. Staff and administrators may need help translating this information to decide what program changes to make and how to adjust the goals and outcome measures accordingly.

Participant Assessment Forms, Operation New Hope (Florida)
Operation New Hope (ONH) is a nonprofit community development corporation that provides case management, life coaching, job training, and job placement services to people released from prisons and jails as part of the Ready4Work Initiative. In partnership with the University of North Florida, ONH developed a comprehensive, 80-question assessment form that populates a database of standardized case files for program participants. The assessment form captures information about a person's demographic background, criminal history, employment history,

*For more information on the Latino Coalition for Faith and Community Initiatives, see www.latinocoalition.org/missionsandgoals.html.

education level, physical and mental health issues, and past and current substance use, among other elements. It also identifies *weighted factors,* or indicators that are most important in identifying the service needs of an individual. Graduate students at the University of North Florida verify information in the database such as recidivism rates for reentry program participants.

ONH staff partner with substance abuse and mental health treatment specialists to review assessment outcomes and determine what programs and treatments will most benefit an individual's transition to the community. The case file database enables ONH to conduct comprehensive quarterly reviews of reentry programs. The University of North Florida also assists ONH staff in analyzing these data continuously, so that improvements can be made to ensure efficient allocation of resources and effective programming.

4 | Determine through impact studies whether, and to what extent, the services provided have had their intended effect.

To assess whether programs and services are positively affecting an individual's transition from prison or jail to the community, states must conduct outcome evaluations. These studies consider both short- and long-term effects of a given program and quantify the benefits of a program.

Policymakers typically are most interested in a program's impact on recidivism, which may be difficult to measure because it is defined and tracked in different ways: as rearrest, reincarceration, or revocations. Furthermore, reliable recidivism research often requires at least a one–three-year study period, making it time-consuming and expensive to complete.

Recidivism is not the only measure of a program's impact. For example, in evaluating an employment program, researchers may track and analyze the number of job interviews that resulted in a job offer, the number of months participants were employed during a given time period, the length of job retention, and the wages participants earned at these jobs. For a housing program, researchers may track the number of months participants lived in a stable housing arrangement, the number of months participants experienced homelessness, and the number of address changes participants had during a given period of time.

Ideally these evaluations would follow an experimental design, which compares, for a particular period of time, a randomly assigned group that receives services and completes a program with a control group that does not receive any services. When this approach is not feasible, researchers may use quasi-experimental design, in which a group of people who did not complete the program but are matched for specific characteristics (such as age, ethnicity, criminal history, and area of residence) are compared with program graduates. The characteristics of the population served are important to detail in any recidivism study, as they can greatly impact the outcomes. An anger management program serving a group of people convicted of felony forgery will likely have very different outcomes than an identical program serving people convicted of assault and battery.

Researchers may also want to collect baseline data that reflect the characteristics of program participants before they start the program. This can help researchers assess the impact of a program by comparing how participants are doing before and after the program intervention. Baseline data may capture such factors as the percentage of participants who are unemployed, their average yearly salary, and the number of criminal convictions.

It is unrealistic for most faith-based and community organizations to conduct impact evaluations because of the resources, time, and expertise required. And even if they did have the qualified researchers within their organization to conduct such studies, their results would lack credibility because they evaluated the effectiveness of their own services.

While state governments do not have a good track record of setting aside the resources necessary to conduct such an evaluation—or waiting for the results—states looking for in-depth statistical analyses of grant programs are encouraged to make the investment in studies that do not appear biased by working with intermediaries, universities, and other third-party organizations to conduct formal evaluations of reentry programs funded by government grants.

Ohio Governor's Office of Faith-Based and Community Initiatives
The Governor's Office of Faith-Based and Community Initiatives (GOFBCI) in Ohio contracted with three local organizations to provide reentry services as part of its Children of Incarcerated Parents program, which seeks to strengthen families, reduce recidivism, and decrease the likelihood that children whose parents have been incarcerated will become incarcerated themselves. To assess the effectiveness of the programs, the GOFBCI set aside a portion of the overall Children of Incarcerated Parents grant funds for conducting program evaluations in partnership with the University of Cincinnati. After conducting a process evaluation at the end of the first year of the grant period, researchers analyzed the impact of the program based on recidivism over a 12- and 24-month follow-up period. Researchers then formulated recommendations for how to improve both the program model and its implementation. These recommendations, along with the impact analyses, were used by policymakers to inform decisions about where to direct funding dollars in the future.

Rigorous evaluations are a critical aspect of any reentry program or initiative and can complement process data that are routinely and efficiently collected by grantees and contractors. Evaluations not only will reveal the need for changes in program design and implementation but also will help policymakers make efficient use of dollars and help ensure the sustainability of programs that can demonstrate their positive impact.

CONCLUSION

POLICYMAKERS AT ALL LEVELS OF GOVERNMENT ARE SHOWING UNPRECEDENTED interest in the record number of people coming out of prisons and jails. This steady increase of individuals released from correctional facilities has serious implications for budgets, public safety, and the stability of neighborhoods disproportionately affected by reentry. In response, there has been much activity by government agencies to implement policies, programs, and initiatives to improve the likelihood that people released from prisons and jails will safely and successfully rejoin communities. For such reentry efforts to be effectual, they largely will depend on the government agencies' ability to establish, develop, and maintain relationships with faith-based and community organizations. State officials, in particular, need to take a leadership role in fostering statewide partnerships and reliable networks with faith-based and community groups that have the capacity to deliver effective services to their reentry population as well as meet standards of performance and accountability.

The goals and recommendations outlined within this guide offer strategies for states to build networks with faith-based and community organizations, simplify pathways to funding support, recognize and understand distinct organizational cultures, tailor responses to the populations who will be served by reentry services, and ensure accountability that will help sustain and improve reentry initiatives. By achieving these goals, state officials can make the most of community resources to help initiate or enhance reentry efforts.

APPENDIX A: ADVISORY GROUP*

Cochairs

Assemblyman Jeffrion Aubry
Chair, Corrections Committee
New York State Assembly

Senator Stephen Wise
Chair, Education Pre-K–12 Appropriations
Committee
Florida State Legislature

Tamela R. Aikens
Community Coordinator
Michigan Prisoner Reentry Initiative

Ira Barbell
Senior Associate
Annie E. Casey Foundation (MD)

Cleveland Bell, III
Executive Director
Riverside House (FL)

Jane B. Brown
Director of Community Partnerships and
Virginia Faith-Based & Community Initiatives
Liaison
Virginia Department of Social Services

J. David Donahue
Commissioner
Indiana Department of Correction

Tommie Dorsett
Program Director
InnerChange Freedom Initiative (TX)

Jonathan E. Ford
Executive Director
Turning the Tide (PA)

Larry W. Gaalswyk
Executive Director
T.E.A.M. Mentoring, Inc. (MT)

Kevin T. Gay
President
Operation New Hope (FL)

Shawn Green-Smith
Community Liaison
Office of the Governor (WI)

Carolyn Harper
Senior Program Officer
Public/Private Ventures (PA)

---

*Advisory group members' titles are reflective of the positions they held at the time of the advisory group meeting in June 2007.

Thomasina Hiers
Director of Programs and Services
Maryland Department of Public Safety
and Correctional Services

Carmen Lingo
Resource Development Assistant
Riverside House (FL)

J. Stephen McCoy
President, Safe Passage Home, Inc.
Senior Pastor, Beaches Chapel (FL)

James R. McDonough
Secretary
Florida Department of Corrections

Peggy A. McGarry
Senior Program Manager
JEHT Foundation (NY)

Katherine McQuay
Senior Policy Analyst
COPS Office
U.S. Department of Justice

Andrea Milani
Director of Re-Entry Services
Talbert House (OH)

Shirley A. Miller
Executive Director
Gracious Promise Foundation (KS)

Andrew Molloy
Sr. Policy Advisor for Corrections
Bureau of Justice Assistance
Office of Justice Programs
U.S. Department of Justice

Tina Naidoo
Program Director
Texas Offenders Reentry Intitiative

Craig Powell
Executive Coordinator
PowerNet of Dayton (OH)

Richard Ramos
President and CEO
Latino Coalition for Faith and Community Initiatives
(CA)

A.J. Sabree
Director of Reentry and Risk Reduction Services
Georgia Department of Corrections

Scott Shortenhaus
Special Assistant,
Center for Faith-Based and Community Initiatives
U.S. Department of Labor

Heidi Soderberg
Executive Director
SE Works (OR)

Jennifer Sordi
Assistant Deputy Superintendent
Hampden County Sheriff's Department (MA)

L. Elaine Sutton Mbionwu
Consultant
Covenant Collaborative Consulting & Training (GA)

APPENDIX B: FOCUS GROUP*

Tamela Aikens
Community Coordinator
Michigan Prisoner Reentry Initiative

Jim Kennedy
Director, Economic Opportunities
Memphis Leadership Foundation

Jack Micklos
Deputy Director
San Diego Second Chance Program

Margie Phelps
Director of Release Planning
Kansas Department of Corrections

David Reyes
Lieutenant
Yuma County Sheriff's Office (AZ)

Anthony Streveler
Policy Initiatives Advisor
Wisconsin Department of Corrections

*Focus group participants' titles are reflective of the positions they held at the time of the focus group meeting in April 2008.

ENDNOTES

1. P.M. Harrison and A.J. Beck, *Prison and Jail Inmates at Midyear 2007*, U.S. Department of Justice, Bureau of Justice Statistics, NCJ221944 (Washington, DC: U.S. Government Printing Office, 2008). Allen J. Beck, "The Importance of Successful Reentry to Jail Population Growth." Presented at the Urban Institute Reentry Roundtable, June 27, 2006, Washington, DC.

2. This study, conducted by the U.S. Department of Justice, examined the rearrest, reconviction, and reincarceration of people discharged from prisons in 15 states three years after their release. P.A. Langan and D.J. Levin, *Recidivism of Prisoners Released in 1994,* U.S. Department of Justice, Bureau of Justice Statistics, NCJ 193427 (Washington, DC: U.S. Government Printing Office, 2002).

3. B.R. Johnson and D.B. Larson, *The InnerChange Freedom Initiative: A Preliminary Evaluation of a Faith-Based Prison Program* (Philadelphia: Center for Research on Religion and Urban Civil Society, University of Pennsylvania, 2003).

4. Safer Foundation, retrieved from www.saferfoundation.org/viewpage.asp?id=324 (accessed August 31, 2007).

5. The *White House Faith-Based and Community Initiatives: Important Contact Information—State Liaisons,* retrieved from www.whitehouse.gov/government/fbci/contact-states.html (accessed September 17, 2007).

6. Robert A. Sudlow (Director, Ulster County Probation Department, NY), personal communication, May 13, 2008.

7. Maureen Janssen (Senior Probation Officer, South Dakota Federal Probation Office), personal communication, June 23, 2008.

8. *Report of the Re-Entry Policy Council,* retrieved from www.reentrypolicy.org/Report/PartI/ChapterI-B/PolicyStatement4/Recommendation4-D#38-note.

9. National Institute on Drug Abuse, *Principles of Drug Abuse Treatment for Criminal Justice Populations: A Research-Based Guide* (Washington, DC: National Institute on Drug Abuse, 2006).

10. Council of State Governments, *Criminal Justice/Mental Health Consensus Project Report* (New York: Council of State Governments, 2002), 293–295.

About the Bureau of Justice Assistance, U.S. Department of Justice

The Bureau of Justice Assistance (BJA), a component of the U.S. Department of Justice, Office of Justice Programs, supports law enforcement, courts, corrections, treatment, victims services, technology, and prevention initiatives that strengthen the nation's criminal justice system. BJA provides leadership, services, and funding to America's communities by:

- emphasizing local control, based on the needs of the field;
- developing collaborations and partnerships;
- providing targeted training and technical assistance;
- promoting capacity building through planning;
- streamlining the administration of grants;
- creating accountability of projects;
- encouraging innovation; and
- communicating the value of justice efforts to decision makers at every level.

    ■ Read more at www.ojp.usdoj.gov/BJA/.

About the Center for Faith-Based and Community Initiatives, U.S. Department of Labor

The work of the Center for Faith-Based and Community Initiatives (CFBCI) at the U.S. Department of Labor (DOL) stems from a simple conviction: Americans can do better for our neighbors in need when we draw upon the unique strengths of every willing partner.

CFBCI works collaboratively with DOL agencies to fulfill the Department's fundamental goal of creating a prepared and competitive, safe and secure American workforce. To accomplish this, CFBCI empowers faith-based and community organizations (FBCOs) that help individuals in their communities prepare for, enter, and thrive in the workforce. CFBCI's goal is to help more Americans overcome barriers to employment, find jobs, and advance in employment through the unique work of local FBCOs. To accomplish this goal, DOL has increased collaboration with both faith- and community-based nonprofit organizations that are trusted institutions providing valuable services, regardless of whether they have a history of partnering with government.

Specifically, CFBCI works to remove administrative and regulatory barriers to FBCO participation in DOL grant programs. It also shapes DOL's community outreach and grant-making policies to utilize the strengths of FBCOs and the role they play in their communities. CFBCI works with various DOL agencies to foster innovative partnerships between DOL-funded programs and FBCOs. Further, CFBCI educates FBCOs about local opportunities to collaborate with government and about opportunities to participate in Federal grant programs. CFBCI also works with public workforce system administrators and staff to integrate FBCOs into their strategic planning and service delivery process.

    ■ Read more at www.dol.gov/cfbci/.

About the Council of State Governments Justice Center

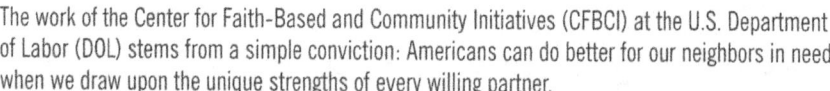

The Council of State Governments (CSG) Justice Center is a national nonprofit organization serving policymakers at the local, state, and federal levels from all branches of government. The CSG Justice Center provides practical, nonpartisan advice and consensus-driven strategies, informed by available evidence, to increase public safety and strengthen communities.

    ■ Read more at www.justicecenter.csg.org.

Council of State Governments
Justice Center

100 Wall Street
20th Floor
New York, NY 10005
tel: 212-482-2320
fax: 212-482-2344

4630 Montgomery Avenue
Suite 650
Bethesda, MD 20814
tel: 301-760-2401
fax: 240-497-0568

504 W. 12th Street
Austin, TX 78701
tel: 512-482-8298
fax: 512-474-5011

www.justicecenter.csg.org